AA

50 WALKS IN

Staffordshire

50 WALKS OF 2–10 MILES

First published 2003
All walks researched and written by
Paul Grogan except 1, 2, 3, 7, 8, 17, which
were contributed by Hugh Taylor and
Moira McCrossan.
Field checked and updated 2009
by Andrew McCloy

Commissioning Editor: Sandy Draper
Senior Editor: Penny Fowler
Designer: Tracey Butler
Picture Research: Vivien Little
Proofreader: Marilynne Lanng
Cartography provided by the Mapping
Services Department of AA Publishing

Produced by AA Publishing
© AA Media Limited 2009

Published by AA Publishing (a trading
name of AA Media Limited, whose
registered office is Fanum House, Basing
View, Basingstoke, Hampshire RG21 4EA;
registered number 06112600)

This product includes
mapping data licensed
from the Ordnance Survey® with the
permission of the Controller of Her
Majesty's Stationery Office. © Crown
Copyright 2009. All rights reserved.
Licence number 100021153.

A03628

ISBN: 978-0-7495-6293-9
ISBN: 978-0-7495-6326-4

A CIP catalogue record for this book
is available from the British Library.

Visit AA Publishing at theAA.com/bookshop

Cover reproduction by Keenes
Group, Andover
Printed by Printer Trento Srl, Italy

Acknowledgements
The Automobile Association wishes to
thank the following photographers and
organisations for their assistance in the
preparation of this book.

Abbreviations for the picture credits are as
follows – (AA) AA World Travel Library

3 AA/C Jones; 9 AA/C Jones; 12/13 AA/C
Jones; 28/29 AA/C Jones; 50/51 AA/C Jones;
64/65 AA/C Jones; 84/85 AA/C Jones; 116
AA/C Jones; 120 AA/C Jones; 140/141 AA/C
Jones

Every effort has been made to trace the
copyright holders, and we apologise in
advance for any accidental errors. We
would be happy to apply any corrections in
the following edition of this publication.

Author Acknowledgement:
Paul Grogan would like to thank John
and Jean for their generous hospitality and
Emma for her unfailingly cheerful support.

Right: Bridge across stream, near Flash Bottom Cathedral (Walk 1)

50 WALKS IN

Staffordshire

50 WALKS OF 2–10 MILES

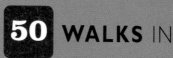

Contents

Contents

Rating

Each walk is rated for its relative difficulty compared to the other walks in this book. Walks marked ✦✦✦ are likely to be shorter and easier with little total ascent. The hardest walks are marked ✦✦✦.

Walking in Safety

For advice and safety tips see page 144.

Locator Map

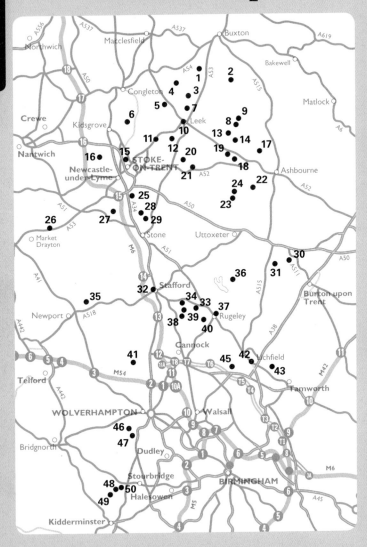

Legend

→⊢	Walk Route		Built-up Area
❶	Route Waypoint		Woodland Area
– – –	Adjoining Path	🚻	Toilet
⧵⏐⫽	Viewpoint	🅿	Car Park
•	Place of Interest	⊞	Picnic Area
⌂	Steep Section	)(	Bridge

Introducing Staffordshire

Did you know that Staffordshire bore the brunt of the largest non-nuclear explosion of World War Two? Or that the county's regiment once boasted within its ranks the most decorated NCO of World War One? Or going back a little further, that George Handel penned his masterpiece, *The Messiah*, on Staffordshire soil? If so, you'll no doubt also be aware that Staffordshire was home to the first canals and the first factory in Britain, that it had front-row seats for the drama surrounding one of the most notorious murder trials of the 19th century, and – more recently – that it provided the scenery and setting for the slightly less macabre television drama *Peak Practice*.

But even the most well versed of Staffordshire aficionados should still be able to find a few novel nuggets in this little volume, if not to entertain and amuse, then at least to inform and educate. Of course, the county's varied culture and interesting history are all well and good, but what of its potential for walking?

In outline, Staffordshire looks not unlike the profile of a man giving Leicestershire a big kiss (have a look if you don't believe me!). The man's forehead to the north-east of the county is arguably the best region for hillwalking as it comprises a significant chunk of the Peak District. This area is characterised by lofty moors, deep dales and tremendous views of both. In fact seven of the walks can be found in this area, from the great crags of the Roaches to the mysterious Thor's Cave. Further south, at around ear level, are the six sprawling towns that make up Stoke-on-Trent, which historically have had such an impact on Staffordshire's fortunes, not to mention its culture and countryside. This is pottery country, formerly at the forefront of the Industrial Revolution and the driving force behind a network of canals that still criss-crosses the county.

In terms of its scenery, the region around Stoke is surprisingly hilly, thanks largely to vast outcrops of limestone not unlike those found in the Peak District just to the north. In areas where industry once marched rampant o'er hill and down dale, mother nature has recently re-staked her claim on the landscape, which today is typified by peaceful wooded valleys, pond-pearled streams and gently rolling hills.

Next up, hanging like an earring from the lobe of Stoke, is Stafford, home to one of the oldest and most impressive castle earthworks in the country. In fact, glancing at some of the other walks in this area, you'd be forgiven for thinking that it's always been a region of conflict, what with the bloody battlefield of Bloreheath just to the west and the enormous Fauld Crater just to the east.

PUBLIC TRANSPORT

Staffordshire is very well served by public transport: First PMT (08708 500868) is one of the main operators in the north-east of the county, while Arriva (www.arrivabus.co.uk) services routes throughout the region. Local bus timetables for most major towns and routes can be obtained from Traveline (0871 200 22 33 or www.traveline.org. uk). To plan your journey online go to www.transportdirect.info.

Just to the south of Stafford is Cannock Chase, arguably the county's best-kept secret. Here, acre after acre of ancient hunting forest has been reclaimed from the devastation wrought by industry to form a huge forested nature park, just a stone's throw from Birmingham. It would take you days, if not weeks, to walk every track in these justifiably popular woods.

And finally, at the southern tip of the county, along the back of our man's neck, are the slopes and ridges that terminate in the impressive vantage point of Kinver Edge, where entire houses are carved into the sandstone cliffs, and where the fine English wine, in a good year, flows freely. Of course, for walking, any year is a good year in Staffordshire.

Using this book

Information Panels

An information panel for each walk shows its relative difficulty (see page 5), the distance and total amount of ascent. An indication of the gradients you will encounter is shown by the rating ▲ ▲ ▲ (no steep slopes) to ▲ ▲ ▲ (several very steep slopes).

Maps

There are 30 maps, covering 40 of the walks. Some walks have a suggested option in the same area. The information panel for these walks will tell you how much extra walking is involved. On short-cut suggestions the panel will tell you the total distance if you set out from the start of the main walk. Where an option returns to the same point on the main walk, just the distance of the loop is given. Where an option leaves the main walk at one point and returns to it at another, then the distance shown is for the whole walk. The minimum time suggested is for reasonably fit walkers and doesn't allow for stops. Each walk has a suggested map.

Start Points

The start of each walk is given as a six-figure grid reference prefixed by two letters indicating which 100km square of the National Grid it refers to. You'll find more information on grid references on most Ordnance Survey maps.

Dogs

We have tried to give dog owners useful advice about how dog friendly each walk is. Please respect other countryside users. Keep your dog under control, especially around livestock, and obey local bylaws and other dog control notices.

Car Parking

Many of the car parks suggested are public, but occasionally you may find you have to park on the roadside or in a lay-by. Please be considerate when you leave your car, ensuring that access roads or gates are not blocked and that other vehicles can pass safely.

Right: Lichfield Cathedral (Walk 42)

Flash Money

Rogues and vagabonds, counterfeiters and bare-knuckle fighters meet the righteous in Britain's highest village.

DISTANCE 6 miles (9.7km)	**MINIMUM TIME** 4hrs
ASCENT/GRADIENT 656ft (200m) ▲▲▲	**LEVEL OF DIFFICULTY** ✦✦✦
PATHS Some on road but mostly footpaths which can be boggy in wet weather	
LANDSCAPE Hills, moorland and meadows	
SUGGESTED MAP OS Explorer OL24 White Peak	
START/FINISH Grid reference: SK 026672	
DOG FRIENDLINESS Suitable for dogs, but keep on lead near livestock	
PARKING On roadside near school	
PUBLIC TOILETS None en route	

At an altitude of 1,518ft (463m), the village of Flash proclaims itself as the 'Highest Village in Britain', and at this elevation winter comes early and lingers past the point where spring has visited its lower neighbours. Winters here can be cold. Once, during wartime, it got so cold that the vicar had icicles on his ears when he ventured from his house to the church. On another occasion a visiting minister arrived by motorcycle, much to the astonishment of the congregation. They were surprised to see him because heavy snow was imminent. They told him to watch for it falling at the window opposite his pulpit and that, should he see any, he should stop the service and depart immediately. Just after he left, it started to snow and within 20 minutes the village was cut off.

Sharp Practice

Despite being a devout community, Flash also has the dubious honour of giving its name to sharp practice. The terms 'flash money' and 'flash company' entered the English language as a consequence of events in Flash. A group of peddlers living near the village travelled the country hawking ribbons, buttons and goods made in nearby Leek. Known as 'Flash men' they initially paid for their goods with hard cash but after establishing credit, vanished with the goods and moved on to another supplier. Their name became associated with ne'er-do-wells in taverns, who helped people drink their money and were never seen again, as typified in the 18th-century English folk-song, *Flash Company*.

> *Fiddling and dancing were all my delight*
> *But keeping flash company has ruined me quite*

Beyond the Law

Flash money on the other hand referred to counterfeit bank notes, manufactured in the 18th century by a devious local gang using button presses. They were captured when a servant girl exposed them to the authorities. Some of the gang members were hanged at Chester.

FLASH

Flash was the ideal location for avoiding the law because of its proximity to the borders of three counties and police in one county could not pursue miscreants into another. At a local beauty spot called Three Shire Heads, about a mile (1.6km) north-west of the village, by a packhorse bridge, is the meeting place of Derbyshire, Cheshire and Staffordshire. Illegal bare-knuckle fights were held here and when the police arrived, the participants simply crossed the bridge and continued their bout on the other side.

While all this lawlessness was going on the more peaceable inhabitants formed the Tea Pot Club. Originally a fund to help members who were unwell, the Flash Loyal Union Society still has an annual Tea Pot Parade, which is held each June, from the church to Flash Bar. Tea is served in the church hall and the person pulling the most grotesque face in the gurning competition wins the grand prize — you've guessed it — a teapot.

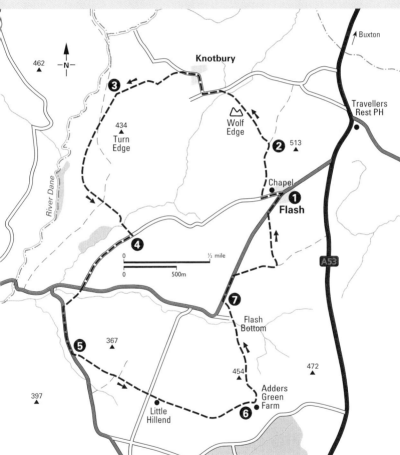

WALK 1 DIRECTIONS

❶ Walk through the village, pass the pub and an old chapel. Turn right at a footpath sign and head towards the last house. Go over a stile, turn right and follow the path over two walls. Veer left towards a gate in the corner of the field to a lane between walls. Cross another stile, then turn left at a waymarker.

Overleaf: Moors above Flash (Walk 1)

1

2 Continue through a gate then follow the waymarker right and uphill to Wolf Edge. Pass the rocks, veer left downhill over a stile and across heather moorland. Cross a stile on the right and continue downhill to a marker post. Cross the wall, then a bridge and turn left on to the road. Go right at the junction and follow this road through Knotbury then, after the last house on the left, take the path on the left, crossing several stiles over the moorland.

WHAT TO LOOK OUT FOR

Look for evidence of the network of packhorse trails on the moors. These routes were used from medieval times to transport goods between communities. Packhorse trains could have anything up to 50 horses and were led by a man called a 'jagger' (their ponies were Galloway cross-breeds called Jaegers). Today you will find their paved routes, descending into the valleys in distinctive 'hollow ways' or sunken lanes. Jaggers drove their beasts across the moors until the early 19th century, when canal transport finally usurped them.

3 Follow this path downhill, go left along a farm track, then resume the downward route through fields and join another track. Veer right off the road at the next waymarker, cross a stile then keep straight ahead at the next signpost. Follow this track until it crosses a bridge, then heads uphill.

4 Opposite Spring Head turn right on to the road. At the junction, turn right then left through a gap stile. Go downhill, over a bridge, then uphill following the path, left across the field, through a gap stile and turn left on the road.

WHERE TO EAT AND DRINK

The Travellers' Rest at Flash Bar is the best place in the area. Walkers can be assured a warm welcome and can relax in front of a fire with a pint of real ale, enjoying the ambience of this fine old building with its flag floors and oak beams.

5 Go left at the next signpost, following the waymarked path to a farm track. At some farm buildings go through a gate and then fork right. Continue to the road, cross it then continue on the path through Little Hillend. Follow this waymarked path to Adders Green Farm.

6 Turn left, through a gate and walk beside a wall. At the end of the wall turn left, follow the wall, cross a gate and then follow the path round the foot of the hill and through a gate to Flash Bottom. Go through a small gate, turn left and up to the driveway. Go through a gate opposite, follow the path over a field and up some steps to reach the road.

7 Turn right, then right again at the next sign. Cross several fields on a well waymarked path towards farm buildings. Cross over a stream then head uphill to the left to rejoin the road back to Flash.

Peak Practice

Ramble over hills and dales in the footsteps of some of television's favourite doctors.

2

> **DISTANCE** 6 miles (9.7km) **MINIMUM TIME** 4hrs
> **ASCENT/GRADIENT** 459ft (140m) ▲▲▲ **LEVEL OF DIFFICULTY** ✦✦✦
> **PATHS** Some on road, otherwise good footpaths, can be muddy
> **LANDSCAPE** Valleys, hills and meadows
> **SUGGESTED MAP** OS Explorer OL24 White Peak
> **START/FINISH** Grid reference: SK 089649
> **DOG FRIENDLINESS** Suitable for dogs but keep on lead near livestock
> **PARKING** Longnor village square
> **PUBLIC TOILETS** Longnor village square

Longnor, a charming Peak village, situated on a high ridge between the Dove and Manifold rivers, developed as a meeting place on the ancient trade routes that once crossed these hills from Sheffield, Chesterfield, Nottingham and the Potteries. More recently it has become famous as the location of the television drama *Peak Practice*, which chronicles the everyday lives of a group of country doctors and their patients. First screened in 1993, the series put the Peak District's magnificent scenery on the television map and has since attracted countless visitors to the area. The earlier episodes took many different parts of the area to establish fictional Cardale – particularly Crich. However, the drama finally established a base in this little Staffordshire village to give the programmes a more permanent, community feel. Real life in Longnor, though, is somewhat quieter than the television version, which ceased filming in 2002.

Familiar Places

There is plenty that will be familiar to viewers of *Peak Practice*. The fine brick frontage of the fictional Cardale Tearoom is actually a Georgian hotel built to serve the needs of the Crewe and Harpur Estate and still retains that name. It was used as a meeting place for the local farmers when they came to pay their annual rents at the end of March. The Horseshoe has the honour of being the TV doctors' local, the Black Swan. Dating back to 1609 it was an important staging point for the packhorse and carriage trade that crossed these hills. Ye Olde Cheshire Cheese, one of two other pubs in the village, had its origins as a cheese store in 1464. It still has a reputation for fine food but its main attraction is its resident ghost, Mrs Robins, a former tenant.

The ancient pubs and cobbled market square are a reminder of Longnor's importance in days gone by as a market town. The turnpike roads with their tolls, and the lack of a railway link, prevented Longnor's development as a major trading centre, but the village retains its Victorian market hall. Now a craft centre and coffee shop, it still has the old market toll charge board, with a list of long-forgotten tariffs, above the front door. However

LONGNOR

Longnor's old world ambience and location at the heart of ancient paths ensures that it is still busy with walkers, cyclists and tourists.

Local Boy

One of the highlights of a visit to Longnor is the churchyard of St Bartholomew's. Although the church is 18th century, the churchyard has some ancient graves, including that of the remarkable William Billings, who lived to the ripe old age of 112. Born in a cornfield, he was at the capture of Gibraltar in 1704, saw action at the Battle of Ramillies in 1706 and fought against the Stuarts in the Jacobite Risings of 1715 and 1745.

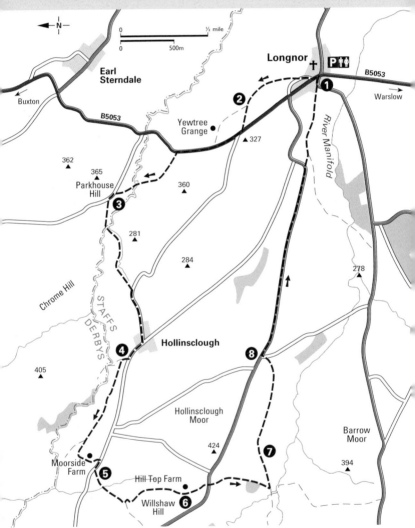

WALK 2 DIRECTIONS

1 From the square take the road towards Buxton. Take the first right to turn into Church Street, then go immediately left, up a lane and right up steps to the footpath. Follow the waymarkers, behind some houses, over a stile and along a wall. Cross another stile, go downhill and turn left on to a farm road.

2 At a fork go left then turn right on to the road. Just before the bend towards the bottom of the hill, take the farm road on the left. At the end, continue through a gate on to the footpath, through a gap stile, downhill, across a bridge and continue straight ahead. Eventually cross a stile and turn left on to the road.

3 Fork left on to a farm road, following the waymarked path. Cross a bridge by a ford and turn left to follow the river bank to the road. Turn right through Hollinsclough, following the road to the right and uphill. Turn right on to a bridleway, through a gate and downhill.

WHERE TO EAT AND DRINK

In Longnor, The Manifold Tea Room and Take Away is a traditional fish and chip shop with indoor seating. The Craft Centre and Coffee Shop, in the former market hall, serves home-made cakes and cream teas. There's also four pubs.

4 After 50yds (46m) fork left by two stones and continue along the flank of the hill. Cross a stile then, at a stone wall, fork left and uphill. At the top turn left at a stone gatepost, through Moorside Farm, through a kissing gate to the road. Turn right then cross a stile to a public footpath on the left.

5 Go downhill to reach a stream and cross a stile to the left of the ditch. Head uphill, through a stile in the wire fence, then through a gap in the wall and round the field to a gap stile. Turn back towards Willshaw Farm, then left on to the

well-signposted footpath towards Hill Top Farm.

6 Follow the path over stiles and past the farm to the road. Go left, then take the farm road on the right. Approaching the farm go right, steeply downhill, over a stile and follow the path along the wall. Just before the stream, cross a stile on the left and head uphill to the left of some trees.

WHAT TO LOOK OUT FOR

Some 350 million years ago, Britain lay south of the equator and the Peak District enjoyed a tropical climate. The Peak limestones were built up over millions of years from the remains of shells, corals and tiny aquatic creatures called crinoids. Parkhouse and Chrome hills on this walk, are limestone reefs, which formed, rather like mud or silt piles, during this period.

7 Continue walking uphill, through a gate in a stone wall to some ruined buildings. Follow the track to the next farm, bear left after the barn, then go left on to a footpath uphill.

WHILE YOU'RE THERE

Well dressing is centuries old. A wooden framework holds a bed of clay, into which flower petals, moss, berries, cones and seeds are pressed in an intricate design. The display is then placed over the well in a special ceremony. Dressings take place throughout the summer.

8 Go through a stile, follow the wall uphill, over two stiles to the road. Turn left then right towards Longnor. Just before the road bends left, cross a stile on the right, go downhill and over several stiles to a farm road. Turn right and follow this road back to the village and your car.

Lud's Church
and the Roaches

Follow Sir Gawain and find the
chapel of the Green Knight.

DISTANCE 6.75 miles (10.9km)	MINIMUM TIME 4hrs
ASCENT/GRADIENT 1,020ft (311m) ▲▲▲	LEVEL OF DIFFICULTY ✦✦✦
PATHS Rocky moorland paths, forest tracks and road	
LANDSCAPE Moor and woodland	
SUGGESTED MAP OS Explorer OL24 White Peak	
START/FINISH Grid reference: SK 005621	
DOG FRIENDLINESS Keep on lead near livestock	
PARKING In lay-by on lane near Windygates Farm	
PUBLIC TOILETS None en route	

The jagged ridge of the Roaches is one of the most popular outdoor locations in the Peak District National Park. The name is a corruption of the French for rocks – *roches*. It was here on the gritstone crags that the 'working class revolution' in climbing took place in the 1950s. Manchester lads, Joe Brown, a builder, and Don Whillans, a plumber, went on to become legends within the climbing fraternity by developing new rock climbing techniques wearing gym shoes and using Joe's mother's discarded clothes line as a rope. Other, less tangible legends, surround this long outcrop, several of them attached to Doxey Pool. Locals speak in hushed voices of a young mermaid, who lived in the pool, but was captured by a group of men. If the stories are to be believed her ghost can still be heard singing through the mist. Lurking in the darkest depths of the pool is Jenny Greenteeth, a hideous monster with green skin, long hair and sharp teeth, who grabs the ankles of anyone unfortunate enough to get too close, dragging them to a deep and watery grave.

Sir Gawain and the Green Knight

But the greatest legend associated with the Roaches is the Arthurian tale of Sir Gawain and the Green Knight. According to the 14th-century poem, a knight on horseback, cloaked entirely in green, gatecrashed a feast at Camelot and challenged the Knights of the Round Table. Sir Gawain rose to the challenge and beheaded the Green Knight but the latter retrieved his head and laughingly challenged Sir Gawain to meet with him again, in a year's time, at the Green Chapel. This has been identified as Lud's Church, near the Roaches. In the 1950s Professor Ralph Elliot, now of the University of Adelaide in Australia, identified the Roaches as the general location of the chapel from the text.

> *Great crooked crags, cruelly jagged, the bristling barbs of rock*
> *seemed to brush the sky*

Professor Elliot's theory was supported by a group of linguists, working on the poem at the same time, who placed the work in the same 15-mile (25km)

THE ROACHES

radius. The professor and a group of students from Keele University, where he was then based, tramped all over the countryside looking for a suitable cave to match the poetic description.

> *A hole in each end and on either side,*
> *And overgrown with grass and great patches*
> *All hollow it was within, only an old cavern*
> *Or the crevice of an ancient crag*

Lud's Church fitted the bill. This rocky cleft was created by a mass of sandstone slipping away from the slope of the hill. It was here that Sir Gawain kept his rendezvous with the Green Knight resulting in that ghostly gentleman losing his head for a second time.

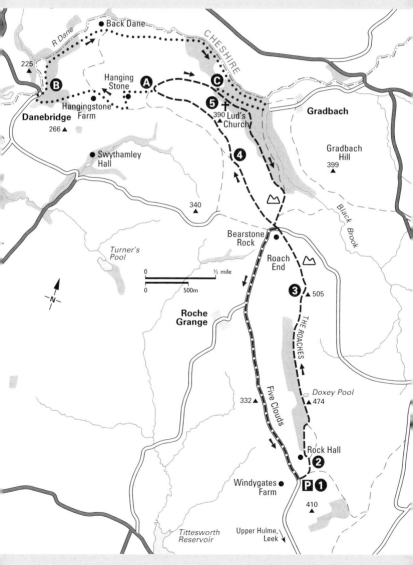

WALK 3 DIRECTIONS

❶ From the lane go through the main gate by the interpretation panel and follow the path half right to the end of the rocks. At a gate in the wall on your right, turn left and straight uphill on a rocky track. Go left through a pair of stone gateposts and continue right on a well-defined track.

WHAT TO LOOK OUT FOR

Look out for Rock Hall cottage built into the rock and containing at least one room that is a natural cave. This listed building is a former gamekeeper's residence, currently owned by the Peak District National Park. Restored in 1989, and now known as the Don Whillans Memorial Hut, the bothy can be booked through the British Mountaineering Council by small groups of climbers.

❷ The path is flanked by rocks on the right and woodland to the left and below. Follow it to the right and uphill through a gap in the rocks. Turn left and then continue uphill. Continue following this ridge path. Pass to the left of Doxey Pool and on towards the trig point.

❸ From here descend on a paved path, past the Bearstone Rock to join the road at Roach End. Go

WHILE YOU'RE THERE

Leek is a magnet for antique hunters. As well as having a host of antique dealers, there's an open-air craft and antique market each Saturday in the historic Market Square. Other markets include the Butter Market, selling mainly fresh traditional produce, on Wednesday, Friday and Saturday. Also worth visiting is the water-powered corn mill at Brindley's Mill.

through a gap in the wall, over a stile and follow the path uphill keeping the wall on the left. At the signpost, fork right on to the concessionary path to Danebridge.

❹ Follow this path keeping straight ahead at a crossroads, go through a wall gate and up towards an outcrop. Carry on along the ridge then head down to a signpost by a gate. Turn right and follow the bridleway signed 'Gradbach'. At the next signpost fork right towards Lud's Church.

WHERE TO EAT AND DRINK

The Roaches Tearoom at Paddock Farm sits beneath the rocky outcrop of Hen's Cloud almost opposite the car parking area. The food is home-made, excellent and there's plenty of it. There's a conservatory overlooking a herb garden and superb views across Tittesworth Reservoir. It's open daily all year.

❺ After exploring Lud's Church continue along the path, through woodland, following the signs for Roach End, eventually taking a paved path uphill. Keep the wall on your left-hand side and at the top, cross a stile on to the gated road and follow this back to the lay-by near Windygates Farm.

Hanging Stone and Danebridge

Extend the walk to Danebridge, taking in Hanging Stone.
See map and information panel for Walk 3

DISTANCE *9.25 miles (14.9km)* **MINIMUM TIME** *6hrs*
ASCENT/GRADIENT *1,247ft (380m)* ▲▲▲ **LEVEL OF DIFFICULTY** +++

WALK 4 DIRECTIONS
(Walk 3 option)

Leaving Walk 3 at Point **A**, turn left signposted 'Swythamley'. Go through the gate and after 50yds (46m), cross a stile up over a dry-stone wall to the right, following the concessionary path to Hanging Stone. Cross the meadow along the faint path to the next stile, after which the path becomes more obvious. At Hanging Stone, go right down steep steps to the inscription that reads:

'Beneath this rock, August 1st 1874 was buried Burk, a noble mastiff black and tan, faithful as woman, braver than man, a gun and a ramble, his heart's desire, with the friend of his life, this Swythamley squire'

Follow the track down to the bottom and turn right, along the wide track to Hangingstone Farm. Just above the farm, the track continues straight on, but the path off to the left should be taken down the hill, through a section of wood. Keep left where a concessionary path goes straight on, then descend across a field and driveway to Danebridge.

At the road, descend right to the bridge, take the path to the right and go over a stile just before the bridge at Point **B**. Follow the

Dane upstream into woods before crossing a stile into a meadow.

Continue along the obvious path before bearing right, up a short rise, to a stile over a fence. Follow the fence left, along a narrow dirt track. Go through two vertical stone posts and come to another stile, followed by two more stone pillars. At Back Dane farmhouse, where the gravel track turns back on itself, continue ahead. Cross the open slope through a wall and, after 200yds (183m), cross a couple of stiles through a wall, then a fence.

Soon after, pass to the right of a farm building, continuing between two fences and then across another stile towards the river. Just after a path comes in from the right you reach a major path junction under a big tree. Go right up the short, sharp slope following signs to Swythamley, and then right again up an easier incline for 0.5 mile (800m). At a rocky outcrop (admire the views from the tops of the rocks) follow signs to Lud's Church, and rejoin Walk 3 at Point **C**.

Rudyard Reservoir

*An exploration of the Victorian tourist spot
that gave Kipling his name.*

5

DISTANCE 4.5 miles (7.2km)	**MINIMUM TIME** 1hr 45min
ASCENT/GRADIENT 180ft (55m) ▲▲▲	**LEVEL OF DIFFICULTY** ✦✦✦
PATHS Gravel bridleways, footpaths and roads, 2 stiles	
LANDSCAPE Lakeside and woodland	
SUGGESTED MAP OS Explorer 268 Wilmslow	
START/FINISH Grid reference: SJ 939611	
DOG FRIENDLINESS Good, but care should be taken near wildfowl	
PARKING Car park at north-east corner of reservoir	
PUBLIC TOILETS Opposite visitor centre at reservoir's south-west corner	

WALK 5 DIRECTIONS

Rudyard Reservoir was built in 1800 to provide an adequate water supply to the region's canals. It wasn't until the second half of the century, however, that it was commercially exploited as a major tourist attraction, thanks to the fast-growing popularity of boating and picnicking among the Victorian middle classes.

In its heyday, the waterfront would have been awash with holiday-makers escaping from the smoggy industrial towns at weekends, with a fun-fair, bandstand and dance floor for the adults, and carousels, slides and swings for the children. Ice skating was popular in the winter, when fairy lights were hung from trees and great fires on the shore enabled night skating and dancing. The reservoir was also the scene of some amazing spectacles. In June 1861, the memorably-named African Blondin walked over the reservoir on a tightrope. (He was a pupil of Jean Francois Gravelet, the Great Blondin, renowned for crossing Niagara Falls on a tightrope.) Then, in June 1877 a poster records that Captain Webb gave a 'representation in miniature of his cross-Channel feat,' swimming the reservoir two years after he became the first person to swim from England to France.

But it was at a Victorian picnic in April 1863 that the reservoir's name was assured its place in literary history, when renowned pottery designer John Lockwood Kipling met his bride-to-be Alice Macdonald. History has it that the courting couple spent much of their time here and were so fond of the memories that they named their first son after the reservoir.

WHERE TO EAT AND DRINK

From Easter to the end of September, the café opposite the visitor centre does snacks and light refreshments, including hot and cold drinks. For those after something more substantial, the bar at the Hotel Rudyard offers a selection of main meals and bar snacks, Tuesday to Sunday evenings, as well as a Sunday lunchtime carvery.

RUDYARD RESERVOIR

Rudyard Kipling was born in Bombay on 30 December 1865 and spent his first five years in India, before being sent to England to stay with a foster family. After finishing his schooling he returned to India to work as a journalist on the *Civil and Military Gazette*, but it was during his spare time that he wrote the first of the poems and stories that would later make him famous. He went on to write many more, including his most famous poem, *If*. Despite his popular and critical success, Kipling declined many of the honours that were offered to him, including a knighthood, Poet Laureateship, and the Order of Merit, but in 1907, aged 42 he accepted the Nobel Prize for Literature.

WALK

5

WHILE YOU'RE THERE

At weekends during the summer, you can hire rowing boats. Alternatively, the Rudyard Lake Steam Railway offers a 3-mile (4.8km) round trip along the side of the reservoir on a mini-gauge railway about half the size of a standard narrow-gauge railway. Steam-hauled trains operate at various weekends throughout the year, including bank holiday weekends, and most weekdays during school holidays. See www.rlsr.org for details.

Access to the car park is along a potholed, gravel bridleway about 0.25 mile (400m) long. From the car park, take the left fork underneath the obvious bridge. Follow the wide, gravel bridleway until it becomes a footpath, with a mini-gauge railway just to the left (see While You're There). Continue towards the end of the reservoir.

Just before you reach the end, just after the Lakeside Loop signal box, is a picnic site up a short track to the right of the main path. After this, cross the head of the reservoir (there's a pay telescope).

From the visitor centre and toilet block, head away from the reservoir up the footpath beside some prominent black railings (not the vehicle drive through the wide gate). At the top is a metalled road. Turn left to reach the Hotel Rudyard, otherwise turn right and then fork left at The Crescent, after which the road becomes a gravel track. Where the track veers right, take the narrow footpath straight ahead (avoiding the private road into the caravan park). Just after the brow of the rise is a junction of two paths; take the more obvious of these down to a metalled road and turn right. Go downhill and left on a path before a private drive. At the far end, turn right on to a road. Continue above the shore until it becomes unsurfaced at Rudyard Lake Sailing Club.

After 400yds (366m) along the wooded path, cross the stile into a clearing with views over the water. The path eases gently uphill to a gate with a chain, which signals your arrival at Cliffe Park Hall, a vast Victorian pile complete with crenellations. Another open stretch becomes a gentle downhill run to a small, surfaced road which should be followed right, back towards the reservoir. Go over the stile beside the cattle grid and continue around the end of the reservoir to the car park.

WHAT TO LOOK OUT FOR

The visitor centre, in an old boathouse, is home to migrating swallows, which build their nests in the roof space above the water. In 2000 it was feared that building work would scare the birds off permanently, but they returned the following year to produce two broods of chicks.

Mow Cop Castle: a Lofty Folly

This walk from historic Mow Cop offers some of the best views to be found anywhere in the county.

9

DISTANCE 6.25 miles (10.1km)   **MINIMUM TIME** 2hrs 30min

ASCENT/GRADIENT 660ft (201m) ▲▲▲   **LEVEL OF DIFFICULTY** +++

PATHS Gravel bridleways, footpaths and roads, 10 stiles

LANDSCAPE Escarpment top, farmland, canal and woodland

SUGGESTED MAP OS Explorer 268 Wilmslow

START/FINISH Grid reference: SJ 856573

DOG FRIENDLINESS Should be kept on lead in fields

PARKING Car park at Mow Cop Castle (closed at dusk)

PUBLIC TOILETS None en route

The tiny village of Mow Cop and the escarpment on which it is perched has a rich and fascinating history that goes back thousands of years. Its prominent position, visible from five counties, made it the perfect spot for a beacon. It's thought that the Romans may have had a watchtower here; it's known they built a road from nearby Astbury to Biddulph, passing over Nick i' th' Hill, which would have brought them very close to Mow Cop. There's also an abundance of coal, millstone grit and limestone in the region, all of which the Romans would have used.

A Chain of Beacons

During the reign of Elizabeth I, beacons were lit throughout the country warning of imminent invasion by the Spanish Armada, and there is little doubt that Mow Cop would have been part of this chain. More recently it has been used as a beacon for special royal events. On 29 July 1981, by order of Buckingham Palace, a chain of beacons was lit to commemorate the wedding of Prince Charles to Diana Spencer. Prince Charles lit the first beacon at Hyde Park before the message was relayed up and down England. A flare from the Wrekin in Shropshire was meant to signal the lighting of Mow Cop beacon, but because of fog the message was relayed by radio.

An 18th-century Folly

Given the village's lofty position, it perhaps comes as no surprise to learn that Mow Cop is famed for its castle which, situated as it is on the massive stone outcrop right at the top of the escarpment, is visible for literally miles around. But this is no ordinary castle and it certainly wasn't built for defensive purposes. In fact it is not a real castle at all, but an elaborate folly made to look like a ruined medieval fortress, as was fashionable at the time. It was built in 1746 by Randle Wilbraham I of Rode Hall as a summerhouse and as a means of enhancing the view from Rode Hall some 2 miles (3.2km) to the west.

For Everyone to Share

The castle's tower and wall (the latter little more than a façade) still present a striking silhouette to the east as well as the west, and would certainly have impressed, or riled, rival landowners on both sides of the border. A century or so after it was built, the owner of nearby Keele Hall claimed that part of the summerhouse was on his land and therefore that part ownership should fall to him. It was eventually ruled that both parties should share the building, but that the public should also have free access. The castle and its surrounds were threatened by excessive quarrying in the 1920s and 30s, but in 1937, after another legal wrangle, the deeds were donated to the National Trust.

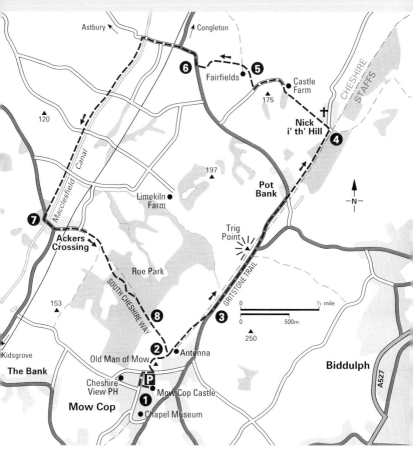

WALK 6 DIRECTIONS

❶ From the castle, turn right along the High Street, then right again up Wood Street. Before you reach the brow of the hill, turn left on the Gritstone Trail to the Old Man of Mow.

❷ Continue along the track to a junction of three paths. Keep ahead, signposted the Gritstone Trail, just to the left of the antenna. Go down steps and at the end of the narrow field take the upper path (not the more obvious lower track) through woodland.

❸ Go left on the metalled road and walk this along the ridge for 0.75 miles (1.2km) until it bends left at Pot Bank Farm. Go straight ahead on the obvious path.

❹ Follow this path until it reaches another road. Turn left down the hill and continue straight down another track, to the left of the Methodist church. Just after a house on the right, the path squeezes through a slot in the wall. Stay straight down through the fields, over the stile. At Castle Farm, go through the gate and follow the road round. After 250yds (229m), after a brick shed on your right, go through a gap in the hedge.

❺ Keeping to the right of Fairfields, cross the stile under a tree and head left across the field to cross a farm driveway. Keeping the same direction, cross a succession of fields and stiles, aiming to the left of the white house in the distance ahead. In the last field, follow the hedge around to the left before crossing another stile on to the road.

❻ Head right along this road, going left on Dodds Lane to cross the railway and then the canal. Drop down to the tow path on the Macclesfield Canal and turn right along it for 1.25 miles (2km).

❼ At Bridge Number 85, cross the canal and, after 200yds (183m), go left up Yew Tree Lane. Go under the railway, keep right at a wide fork, and after 300yds (274m) take a left fork up a steep track and, soon after, the less obvious track, right, into a field. Head right of the farm and follow the hedge up. At the top, cross a stile into the wood.

❽ At the top of the wood, cross another stile into a field and continue to the top of the ridge. Turn right and make your way back past the Old Man and into Mow Cop.

Birds, Beasts and Butterflies at Tittesworth

Reservoir biodiversity provides drinking water for the Potteries and a valuable habitat for wildlife.

7

DISTANCE *4.5 miles (7.2km)* **MINIMUM TIME** *3hrs*

ASCENT/GRADIENT *131ft (40m)* ▲▲▲ **LEVEL OF DIFFICULTY** ✦✦✦

PATHS *Good, well-made footpaths, forest tracks and roads*

LANDSCAPE *Reservoir and woodland*

SUGGESTED MAP *OS Explorer OL24 White Peak*

START/FINISH *Grid reference: SK 994602*

DOG FRIENDLINESS *Suitable for dogs*

PARKING *Reservoir visitor centre (pay car park)*

PUBLIC TOILETS *At reservoir visitor centre*

Tittesworth Reservoir and dam were built in 1858 to collect water from the River Churnet and provide a reliable water supply to Leek's thriving textile and cloth-dying industry. By 1963 work to increase its size had been completed and local farmland was flooded to create a reservoir capable of supplying drinking water to Stoke-on-Trent and surrounding areas. With a capacity of 6.5 billion gallons (29.5 billion litres), when full it can supply 10 million gallons (45 million litres) of water every day.

Habitat for Wildlife

The land around the reservoir provides a habitat for a wide variety of wildlife and many creatures can be seen in the course of this walk. Look out for brown hares in the fields near the car park. You can tell them from rabbits by their very long legs, black-tipped ears and a triangular black and light brown tail. Otters were once hunted almost to extinction by dogs and although the sport is now illegal, their numbers remain low. They are nocturnal creatures and not often seen, but look out for their droppings by the water's edge and the tell-tale prints of their webbed feet and wavy line tail prints in the sand and soft mud. Look also for holes in the banks along the River Churnet, where it enters the reservoir. Although he's a difficult little creature to spot, a hole may just be the entrance to a vole burrow and home to a water vole like Ratty from *The Wind in the Willows*.

Bats and Birds

Europe's smallest bat, the pipistrelle, suffered a severe decline in numbers in the last decades of the 20th century due to loss of hunting habitats like hedges, ponds and grassland. Pond restoration near Churnet Bay is encouraging their return and they can best be seen here near dusk, flying at an incredible speed, twisting and turning as they dive to gobble caddisflies, moths and gnats.

Bird life around the reservoir is also abundant and there are two bird hides from which visitors can observe in comfort. Look out particularly for skylarks, small birds with a high-pitched continuous warble, that nest in the

Overleaf: Tittesworth from The Roaches (Walk 7)

TITTESWORTH RESERVOIR

meadows around Tittesworth. The song thrush, another bird that has been in decline, also finds a home here, as does the linnet. Look especially for the male of the species in spring and summer when it has a bright blood-red breast and forehead. You'll find them in the trees and bushes near the visitor centre and at the hide near the conservation pool.

At various times of the year you might spot barnacle geese, great crested grebe, pied flycatchers, spectacular kingfishers, cormorants and even a rare osprey that has visited here several times in recent years.

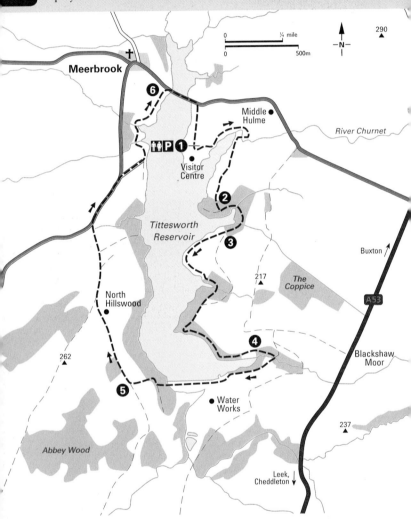

WALK 7 DIRECTIONS

❶ Facing the entrance to the visitor centre turn left, cross the car park and follow the path signed 'Waymarked Walks and Play Area'. Beyond the Nature Trails

sign, continue along the concrete path around the edge of the reservoir. Cross two bridges and follow the Long Trail/Short Trail signs along a well-surfaced path. At a junction by a picnic table turn left on to a forest trail.

TITTESWORTH RESERVOIR

2 Follow the waymarked Long Trail through the wood, crossing a bridge and some duckboarding, then turn left at a T-junction again following the Long Trail (follow footprint waymarks). As the path leaves the wood, fork right on to a grassy track.

3 Continue along the bank of the reservoir then re-enter woodland, cross some duckboards and rejoin the broad, hard-surface track. Cross a bridge by a picnic table, ascend some steps and continue along duckboards. Skirt the edge of a wood, keeping the fence on your left, then go downhill through a wood and along the reservoir bank.

4 Go through some more woodland, cross a bridge, walk up some steps then leave the wood and continue on a gravel path. Follow the path downhill towards the dam. Go through a gate and cross the dam head. At the far end, go uphill on a series of steps and turn right on to a footpath.

5 Go through a gate, turn right at a T-junction on to a metalled lane. Continue on this through a farm, following the signs for Meerbrook, straight ahead. At the road junction turn right at the Long Trail and Visitor Centre sign. Turn right again following the pedestrian-only road to Tittesworth Reservoir. When this turns to the right, bear left on a footpath beside the reservoir.

6 Go through a gate on to the road then turn right into the public entrance to the reservoir to return to the visitor centre.

Along the Manifold Way

Follow the former Manifold Valley, route of one of England's most picturesque small railways.

8

DISTANCE 5.5 miles (8.8km)	**MINIMUM TIME** 3hrs 30min
ASCENT/GRADIENT 518ft (158m) ▲▲▲	**LEVEL OF DIFFICULTY** ✦✦✦
PATHS Hard surface on Manifold Way, other footpaths can be muddy in wet weather	
LANDSCAPE Woodland, meadows and valleys	
SUGGESTED MAP OS Explorer OL24 White Peak	
START/FINISH Grid reference: SK 095561	
DOG FRIENDLINESS Keep on lead near livestock	
PARKING On Manifold Way near Wetton Mill	
PUBLIC TOILETS Next to Wetton Mill Tea Room	

Described by one local as 'A line starting nowhere and ending up at the same place', the narrow gauge Leek and Manifold Valley Light Railway was one of England's most picturesque white elephants. Though it survived a mere 30 years from its first run in June 1904, its legacy is still enjoyed today. It ran for 8 miles (12.9km) from Hulme End to Waterhouses where passengers and freight had to transfer to the standard gauge Leek branch of the North Staffordshire Railway.

The Leek and Manifold Valley Light Railway

The narrow gauge railway owed its existence to Leek businessmen who feared that their town would lose out because of the newly opened Buxton-to-Ashbourne line. Their solution was to provide a local rail link to the south-east of the county. For the entire period of its existence, the railway was a financial disaster and should probably never have been built. It was only made possible because the Light Railways Act of 1896 provided grants for small projects like this and reduced bureaucracy.

A Little Bit of India in the Peaks

Engineer Everard Calthorp, who built the Barsi Railway near Bombay, used the same techniques and design of locomotive for the Leek and Manifold Valley Light Railway in the Peak District as he used in India, and as a result it looked more like a miniature Indian railway than a classic English line. The engines were painted chocolate and black and pulled carriages of primrose yellow.

Milk Train

The success of the line was, however, based on the supposition that the Ecton Copper Mines would re-open and that an extension to Buxton would tap into a lucrative tourist market. But the mines didn't re-open and the extension was never built. To survive, the small railway made a daily collection of milk from farms along the line and hauled produce from the creamery at Ecton for onward transportation to London. Passenger traffic was light, probably due to the long distance and steep uphill climb from the valley bottom to the villages on the top. Tourists did flock to the area on summer weekends and bank holidays, often causing severe overloading of the carriages as they headed for scenic areas like Thor's Cave and Beeston Tor. Even with this seasonal upturn the line never made a profit and when the creamery shut in 1933, it was the end of the road for the miniature trains. The last one ran on 10 March 1934.

The track was lifted and the bed presented by the railway company to Staffordshire County Council. They had the remarkable foresight and imagination to be one of the first local authorities to take a disused railway line and convert it to a pedestrian path. Today, as the Manifold Way, it is a favourite of walkers and cyclists.

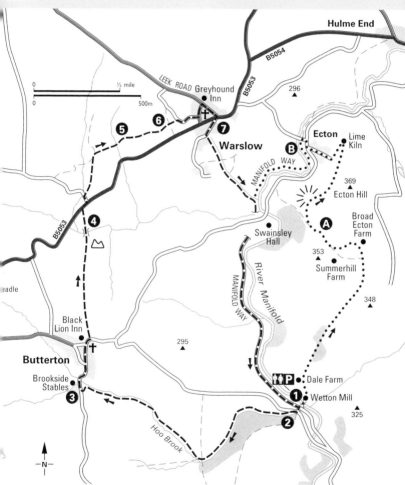

WALK 8 DIRECTIONS

1 At the road junction near the car park, take the lane signposted 'Butterton' opposite the bridge. Just after the road bends sharply right near the ford, go through a gate on the left and walk along a valley-bottom track, with the brook on your left.

2 Beyond the new footbridge turn right at the signpost 'Fp (footpath) to Butterton' and follow this along the course of a stream to reach the village. In the final field go left, uphill, to reach the road.

WHILE YOU'RE THERE

Visit the old station at Hulme End. Now the Manifold Valley Visitor Centre, it has excellent displays covering the history of the Leek and Manifold Valley Light Railway and the industries and communities it served. There are also several relics from the day of steam and a scale model of the line with Hulme End Station as it was in its heyday.

3 Turn right onto the road, cross the ford and then head uphill, forking right to go past the church and the Black Lion Inn. Turn right at a T-junction, go left at a public footpath sign, cross two stiles then head along a spur, through some trees and down a steep hill to cross the stream by a wooden bridge.

4 Head uphill keeping the hedge on your left, cross two stiles and turn right on to the road. Turn left towards Eckstone, then right

WHERE TO EAT AND DRINK

The Black Lion Inn in the nearby village of Butterton is the ideal spot to relax after a day's walking. Built in 1782 this atmospheric, country hostelry has low beams and roaring open fires. Children, dogs and walkers are especially welcome and there is a wide range of food available including a selection for vegetarians. Real ales on tap include Morland Old Speckled Hen and Theakston Black Bull Bitter.

across a stile on to the footpath. Cross two stiles, turn right behind a small derelict building and follow the line of the wall. Cross a stile, then a stream and head uphill keeping the fence on your left.

5 At the junction where the fence meets with a stone wall, turn right, cross the field and nip over a stile by a large tree. Follow this path across a field through a gateway and ahead across marshy ground to a junction of paths in the corner of the field where the wall meets the hedge.

6 Go over a stile and keep ahead through the next field to emerge on the road by Shorecroft Barn. Turn right, then at the end, opposite the church, go left. When you reach the T-junction, turn right on to Leek Road.

WHAT TO LOOK OUT FOR

The walk passes through a tunnel that served the old railway. This is close to Swainsley Hall, which was the home of the Wardle family at the time of construction. They were shareholders in the company building the railway line and although happy to take any profits going, they did not want to be troubled by seeing the trains from their house.

7 Turn right again at the next junction, cross over the road and then walk down School Lane. Turn left through a gap stile on to a public footpath. Clamber through three more gap stiles, following the course of a stream. Enter a wooded area, go downhill, cross over a stile and then turn right to join the Manifold Way. Follow this easy, well-defined trail through an old railway tunnel, back to the car park.

To the Heady Heights of Ecton Hill

As an alternative, climb the hills to the east for magnificent views over the Peaks, then drop down to join the Manifold Way.
(See map and information panel for Walk 8)

9

DISTANCE *4 miles (6.4km)* **MINIMUM TIME** *2hrs*

ASCENT/GRADIENT *900ft (274m)* ▲▲▲ **LEVEL OF DIFFICULTY** +++

WALK 9 DIRECTIONS
(Walk 8 option)

From the car park, Point **❶**, cross the bridge over the river and bear left up a wide gravel track. Proceed through Dale Farm and over the stile, continuing up the middle of the gently sloping valley. When the path reaches the woods, veer left at the waymark post as the ground steepens significantly. Cross the stile after the woods, before making a dog-leg right then left, through a narrow slot in the dry-stone wall. Carry on up this shallow valley, heading right along the faint trail to the gap between the trees.

After the gap, head for the corner of a dry-stone wall and continue up the path. At the gate turn left along the rough road. Just before the farm straight ahead, follow the signs to Summerhill and Lime Kiln. Cross over the stone stile, following the track. At the top left corner of this field, go through the gate and continue straight up the slope, keeping the dry-stone wall to your right. Go through the gap in the dry-stone wall at the top, heading diagonally right to the obvious corner of two walls, Point **❹**.

From the corner, bear left in the direction of the wall and go down the other side of the hill. Cross the obvious stile and drop down 30 paces until you reach a path skirting right around the hill. Follow this path until it rounds an obvious corner. Follow the path to the top of a scree slope surrounded by a small horseshoe of trees.

Above the scree, just to the right of the track, is a well-preserved mineshaft entrance with a red metal gate set into the exposed rock. A small, lone tree provides an ideal spot for a rest before continuing to the conical stone building (Lime Kiln) straight ahead. From the kiln, walk down the steep, grassy slope (take care here, boots or trainers with good grip are recommended) keeping the dry-stone wall to your right. At the bottom of this clearing are a stone stile and some steps leading to the courtyard of an impressive and rambling old building. Follow the track down to the road, then head right, then left to join the Manifold Way, Point **❸**, back to the car park.

Leek Legacy

An 18th-century watermill provides the starting point for a revolution in transportation.

DISTANCE 4.25 miles (6.8km)	**MINIMUM TIME** 1hr 30min
ASCENT/GRADIENT 420ft (128m) ▲▲▲	**LEVEL OF DIFFICULTY** +++
PATHS Meadow track and some road, 12 stiles	
LANDSCAPE Hillside meadow and woodland	
SUGGESTED MAP OS Explorer 258 Stoke-on-Trent	
START/FINISH Grid reference: SJ 977569	
DOG FRIENDLINESS Must be kept on lead at all times	
PARKING Ample roadside parking on Abbey Green Road	
PUBLIC TOILETS None en route (nearest in Leek town centre)	

WALK 10 DIRECTIONS

Leek is an ancient market town that has long been associated with the textile industry. These days, the silks for which it was once renowned have largely been replaced by synthetic alternatives, although a number of textile manufacturers and factory shops selling brand names direct to the public still remain. But it's a little corn mill on the outskirts of the town, built by an illiterate millwright, that put Leek right at the forefront of the Industrial Revolution.

James Brindley was born at Tunstead, near Buxton in Derbyshire, in 1716 and in 1726 his family moved to Leek. Until the age of 17 he worked as a farm labourer and there is no evidence as to what,

if any, formal education he received. He was apprenticed to millwright Abraham Bennett and after nine years of learning his trade he set up on his own as a millwright in Leek. It was here that he designed and built the water-powered corn mill that today houses a museum to his life and work.

However, it wasn't as a millwright that Brindley would make his name, but as a designer and builder of canals. In 1759 the Duke of Bridgewater hired him to devise a system whereby coal could be inexpensively transported from the duke's mines at Worsley to a textile manufacturing centre in Manchester. Brindley's solution was a 10-mile (16.1km) canal that included an underground channel and an aqueduct.

The scale and complexity of the project was unprecedented and when the Bridgewater Canal was completed in 1765, it revolutionised the way goods were transported in the north of England. In short, the age of the canal had begun. Brindley went

---

WHERE TO EAT AND DRINK

The Abbey Inn has a splendid stone patio, overlooking Abbey Green and the Churnet Valley, and a warm, cosy interior. Bar snacks and traditional pub meals are served every lunchtime and evening (closed all day Tuesday).

on to engineer the Trent and Mersey Canal, the Staffordshire and Worcestershire Canal and many others.

In total, he was responsible for 360 miles (579km) of canals, all of which had a huge impact on both the local and national economies. And, as if his career as a millwright and canal engineer weren't impressive enough, he undertook all of his engineering feats without any written calculations or drawings, preferring instead to do everything in his head.

> **WHILE YOU'RE THERE**
>
> Make sure you take a little time to visit St Edward's Church. It boasts a fine 13th-century roof in which every beam has been hewn from a separate oak tree. Leek's market is held every Wednesday in the Market Place, while the Butter Market is open Friday and Saturday.

From the museum turn left along the A523, and immediately left again along Abbey Green Road. Follow this, bearing left over a bridge, to Abbey Green. At The Abbey Inn, turn right through the car park and go up the obvious path. After 30 paces, cross a stile and walk diagonally left to the top of the slope.

At the top bear right, keeping the fence about 20 paces to your left. Proceed through a gate into Abbey Wood where the path becomes wider. After another kissing gate carry on up the bridleway until it becomes a grassy track. Aim just to the left of a small copse ahead. Continue to a slot in the wall at the corner of Back Hills Wood.

Follow the faint track, keeping the dry-stone wall just to your right. At the bottom of the hill go through a

gate and bear slightly left, keeping North Hillswood Farm to your right. At a rough surfaced road, go left until you reach a metalled road. Turn left and 100yds (91m) after Folly Rest, cross a stile on the left. Descend, keeping the fence to your left and at the bottom head right.

Go over the stile and pick your way along the path through Ramshaw Wood. At the top right-hand corner, cross the stile and keep going straight, keeping the bank of trees to your right. At the end of these trees turn left along the bridleway and retrace your steps back to Abbey Green.

Opposite Abbey Dairy go right, over a stile, for a waymarked field path and continue in the same direction over a succession of stiles. After the second stile head diagonally left along the faint track through the meadow to its far right corner. Cross a stile and continue with a fence just to your left. Go through a hedge and up a short hill. At the top, cross a stile to your left and descend, now with the hedge and fence to your right.

At the bottom, cross the stile and head right past the house. At a metalled road, go left, and then left again along the A523, back to Brindley Mill.

> **WHAT TO LOOK OUT FOR**
>
> Brindley Mill is a water-powered corn mill with a riverside garden. It illustrates James Brindley's talents as an architect and a millwright and has a small museum dedicated to his life. Open weekends from Easter to end of September, 2–5pm and some weekdays in July and August.

10

Well Dressed in Endon in the Spring

A short, pleasant walk exploring a Staffordshire village with an ancient and colourful tradition.

DISTANCE 3.5 miles (5.7km)	**MINIMUM TIME** 1hr 30min
ASCENT/GRADIENT 269ft (82m) ▲▲▲	**LEVEL OF DIFFICULTY** ✚✚✚
PATHS Easy meadow paths and some roads, 17 stiles	
LANDSCAPE Hillside meadow, forest and farmland	
SUGGESTED MAP OS Explorer 258 Stoke-on-Trent	
START/FINISH Grid reference: SJ 928537	
DOG FRIENDLINESS Must be kept on lead at all times	
PARKING St Luke's Church car park (Saturdays only) otherwise roadside	
PUBLIC TOILETS None en route	

The name Endon means 'place where lambs are reared', but today the village is best known, not for its mutton, but for its water. The area around Endon, and in fact most of Derbyshire and northern Staffordshire, features an abundance of natural springs. These springs owe their existence to the local geology. The primarily limestone landscape of the Staffordshire moorlands and the rest of the Peak District is intermittently overlaid by a layer of gritstone. As the latter is a non-porous rock, when the water table rises higher than the limestone, water is forced out at the points on the surface where the two rock layers meet. This constant supply of fresh water was doubtless what prompted ancient peoples to settle in the area.

The Black Death

These early settlers began blessing this water supply by adorning local wells with flowers, a ritual known today as well dressing. Its origins are shrouded in mystery: many sources attribute the practice to the period of the Black Death (1348–9) when it's thought that a third of the country's population died of the virus. Some villages remained untouched and, probably quite rightly, attributed this to the clean water supply drawn from their wells. (The plague was borne by rats and their fleas, so dirty water and poor sanitation contributed to the spread of the disease.) However, it's possible that the custom goes back further, perhaps to Celtic times, and the fact that many well dressings have a 'well queen' suggests echoes of ancient fertility rites and rituals.

Well Dressing

Today, well dressing is an annual tradition unique to the central and southern Peak, with a succession of villages dressing their wells between the end of May and early September. Endon's ceremony, which was revived in 1845, traditionally takes place on the spring bank holiday, when two wells are dressed in an elaborate ceremony.

Intricate Pictures

The well dressing itself is usually as intricate as it is elaborate. It is achieved by making a picture, often of a religious theme, out of flowers and petals. The picture is created within a wooden frame filled with soft, wet clay. An outline of the drawing is made using bark, twigs and berries before the spaces are filled in with coloured petals. The picture is made from the bottom upwards so that the petals overlap and rainwater drains off. The finished image is often so ornate it really has to be seen to be believed.

Because of the nature of the materials, dressings have to be made in the two or three days just before the ceremony, and they usually only last a week or so. In addition, a well dressing queen is crowned and, on the Bank Holiday Monday, a fair is held in the village, complete with parade, morris dancing and a tossing the sheaf competition.

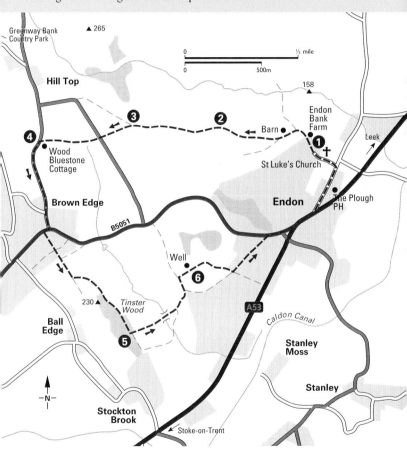

WALK 11 DIRECTIONS

1 From St Luke's Church follow the lane uphill. At the top go right, through the gate for Endon Bank Farm, and after a second join a wide track ahead/left. Follow the track round to the left and, 50yds (46m) after a barn on the right, go through a slot in the wall. Cut off the corner of the field to reach a stile and maintain this direction to reach a double stile on the far side.

WHERE TO EAT AND DRINK

The Plough is conveniently located on the A53 right in the middle of Endon. Standard bar snacks and pub food are available seven days a week and a popular carvery is served Monday to Saturday before 7pm and all day Sunday, all year round.

2 Continue in the same direction, keeping a hedge just to your left. Cross the stile at the far side of the field and proceed to another stile straight ahead. Keep following a tumbledown dry-stone wall to your left until you reach a well-hidden slot in the top left corner of the wall. Continue up the slope, this time with the hedge to your right.

WHAT TO LOOK OUT FOR

Despite the reverence in which some wells are clearly held, many are seen only as marks on a map, often existing below the surface. When they do spring up, they're often indicated by little more than a tap, or in some cases, an algae-stained bath tub!

3 At the top right corner of this field, go straight across the stile and continue along the rough track to a road. Go straight over and across a pair of stiles, following a hedge on the left.

Cross yet more stiles, aiming for the far left corner of the field by Wood Bluestone Cottage.

4 Turn left down the road and, at the junction with the B5051, go right then first left along a signed footpath, over a residential road and up a wide, fenced track. Stay on this as it curves left to the top of the hill and then continues down and along the edge of Tinster Wood. As soon as the track enters the wood proper, head sharp left down a narrow path, somewhat indistinct in places, following it to the bottom left-hand corner.

5 Go through a slot in the wall to your left. Continue straight across a field, keeping the wall to your right, through a pair of wall slots. Cross the small footbridge beneath a tree before crossing a field. At a kissing gate go left up a walled track and left along the road. After 100yds (91m) go right following the footpath sign beside woodland.

6 At the bottom of this field go through a gate to a surfaced road, following it round to the left. When you reach a proper residential road, go hard left along a rougher track to a surfaced road. Head right and, shortly after, turn left along the A53. Just before you get to The Plough on the left, head left up the road signed to St Luke's Church.

WHILE YOU'RE THERE

Greenway Bank Country Park, just to the north-west of Endon, features an arboretum, picnic sites and 114 acres (46ha) of secluded forest around Serpentine Pool and Knypersley Reservoir. A weekend visitor centre provides more local information.

Cheddleton Flint Mill and Deep Hayes

A short walk discovering the parts water and flint have played in the Staffordshire potteries.

DISTANCE 3.25 miles (5.3km)	**MINIMUM TIME** 1hr 30min
ASCENT/GRADIENT 272ft (83m) ▲▲▲	**LEVEL OF DIFFICULTY** ✦✦✦

PATHS Tow path, field and woodland paths (can be muddy), 14 stiles

LANDSCAPE Canal, reservoir, forest and farmland

SUGGESTED MAP OS Explorer 258 Stoke-on-Trent

START/FINISH Grid reference: SJ 961533

DOG FRIENDLINESS Can be off lead along tow path

PARKING Deep Hayes Country Park visitor centre

PUBLIC TOILETS Deep Hayes Country Park visitor centre

The walk starts at Deep Hayes Country Park, a recreational area which has been created around a disused reservoir. The reservoir itself was built in 1849 to compensate the River Churnet for the loss of water to several mills further downstream, while at the same time works were completed at nearby Wall Grange to pump 1.5 million gallons (6.8 million litres) of drinking water from Caena's Well. During the 1830s and 40s thousands died in cholera epidemics because of poor water, so clean water was needed to serve the growing population of the booming Potteries region.

Former Reservoir

The reservoir at Deep Hayes was formed behind an earth dam 50ft (15m) high and 400ft (122m) long, which was built by hand. It continued to 'top up' the River Churnet until as recently as 1979, when problems with the dam's structure became too costly to repair. The water level was reduced, and three separate pools were made to create the country park you see today, complete with trails, toilets and visitor centre.

The Flint Mill

The highlight of the walk, though, is undoubtedly the flint mill on the Caldon Canal. Originally a corn mill dating as far back as the 13th century, it was strengthened for flint grinding in 1800. Flint is a hard, nearly pure form of silica; when ground down to a fine powder it's used to harden and whiten pottery (before flint was used, silica was added in the form of fine sand, but the sand was often iron-stained and impure).

The Production Process

The flint arrived by narrowboat. It was heated in kilns at 1,100 degrees centigrade (2,012 degrees Fahrenheit) to make it more brittle, a process known as 'calcining'. The heated flint was then broken up and ground into fine powder by the water-powered, and later steam-driven, millstones. The slip, a mixture of water and fine flint powder, would be dried into blocks called 'cake' and taken to the wharf for dispatch to the potteries.

Grinding On

The mill continued to be worked well into the 20th century. During World War II, George Edwards & Son ground rutile (a black or reddish-brown mineral) for welding rods and, as late as the 1960s, ceramic stains were ground here for potteries overseas (in Saudi Arabia and Finland, for example). The mill finally stopped grinding flint in 1963.

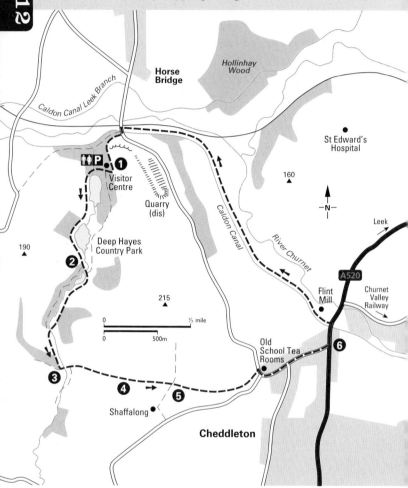

WALK 12 DIRECTIONS

1 From the visitor centre in Deep Hayes Country Park go down to the bottom of the car park and cross the stream before following the shore of the reservoir along a wooded track. The path gains some height above the reservoir, but continues along the shoreline. After the second reservoir and at a fork of two obvious footpaths go left down some steep steps and across the concrete stepping stones.

2 Once across the stream head right through a fence gap with a sign that says 'Keep dogs on leads'. After a short while this track runs alongside the small stream that fills the reservoirs. When you cross

WHERE TO EAT AND DRINK

The Old School Tea Rooms offers a fantastic range of food and drinks, from main meals through to snacks and cakes, home-made soup, freshly made sandwiches and baguettes, as well as an all day brunch. Try the house speciality, Staffordshire oatcakes with a variety of fillings. There is also a small craft centre here, which sells an amazing array of locally produced gifts, including pottery, paintings, photography and needlework. Open Wednesday–Sunday, 10am–4pm, all year round.

back over the stream, continue to follow the stream to the left through an aluminium kissing gate and along a boardwalk.

❸ At a path junction (marked by a wooden signpost) head down steps left, back over the stream for the final time, before following the public footpath sign to Cheddleton. After crossing a stile, go right for 30yds (27m) before continuing up the hill along a wooded trail. At the top of the wood cross the stile and head straight across the field, aiming for the left of the farm buildings called Shaffalong.

❹ In the far corner of the field go along the muddy farm track to a gate. From here follow the obvious, waymarked path over a succession of stiles through a series of small fields to the left of the farm buildings.

❺ Beyond a double stile and a plank footbridge, by a wooden public footpath sign, head straight across the field following the line of trees to your left. After the final tree veer right and cross the small stile over a dry-stone wall and dropping downhill cross the next field to its far side. Just to the left of a clump of trees is a stile followed in quick succession by another stile and a slot in the wall, bringing you out on to the road into Cheddleton almost opposite the tea rooms.

WHAT TO LOOK OUT FOR

The Caldon Canal, running from Froghall to Etruria Junction on the Trent and Mersey Canal in Stoke-on-Trent, was the brainchild of canal-building genius James Brindley. Flint came from Cheddleton on the Caldon Canal, while high-quality clay came from the West Country, via the Mersey and the Trent and Mersey Canal.

❻ When you reach the end of this road, head left, with care, along the A520 and, after 100yds (91m), turn left following signs to the flint mill. After exploring the mill museum, keep going along the canal tow path for about 1 mile (1.6km) until you reach a bridge (number 39) over the canal. Cross over the bridge, before turning right, along the driveway, to return to the visitor centre.

WHILE YOU'RE THERE

The Churnet Valley Railway runs from Cheddleton to Froghall and back again on various dates throughout the year (up to five days a week in summer). All trips are steam-powered in lovingly restored locomotives, and stop at Consall and Leek in addition to Cheddleton and Froghall. All stations have a nearby tea room or pub for a bite to eat, in addition to other attractions, such as the museum and engine shed at Cheddleton, idyllic canal walking at Consall and the Brindley Mill Museum at Leek (see Walk 10). For a timetable, visit Cheddleton Station or www.churnet-valley-railway.co.uk.

In the Lair of the White Worm

*Follow a fascinating limestone trail to visit the film
location of Bram Stoker's last nightmare.*

DISTANCE 5 miles (8km)	**MINIMUM TIME** 3hrs 30min
ASCENT/GRADIENT 423ft (129m) ▲▲▲	**LEVEL OF DIFFICULTY** +++

PATHS Forest tracks, grass and mud, hard footpath

LANDSCAPE Hillside, valley, meadows and woodland

SUGGESTED MAP OS Explorer OL24 White Peak

START/FINISH Grid reference: SK 085545

DOG FRIENDLINESS Keep on lead near livestock

PARKING At Grindon church

PUBLIC TOILETS None en route

Anyone who has seen Ken Russell's film, *The Lair of the White Worm* (1988), will recognise at once the entrance to Thor's Cave and may, as a result, feel slightly apprehensive when climbing the path up the hillside. The opening shot in the film features the famous landmark and, as the blood red titles roll, the camera slowly zooms in towards the mouth of the cave.

Scene of a Horror Film

Based loosely on Bram Stoker's last novel, *The Lair of the White Worm* stars Amanda Donahoe, Hugh Grant, Catherine Oxenburg, Peter Capaldi and Sammi Davis. Stoker's original story was based in the Peak District in the 19th century and tells of odd disappearances, legends of a fearsome giant serpent and of the strange and sinister Lady Arabella. Film-maker Russell moved the whole story in time to the 20th century and altered the plot considerably.

A young Scottish archaeology student, Angus Flint (played by Peter Capaldi) finds a mysterious, reptilian skull at an excavation he's working on near his lodgings. Later he takes the two sisters who run the guest house to the home of Lord James D'Ampton (Hugh Grant) for the annual celebrations to commemorate the slaying of the D'Ampton Worm by his ancestor. Angus leaves early to escort one of the sisters (Mary, played by Sammi Davis) home.

Passing through woods near where her parents mysteriously disappeared they encounter the sensuous and snakelike Lady Sylvia (irresistibly portrayed by Amanda Donahoe). In the dark cellars of her Gothic mansion, Temple Hall, she has been worshipping an evil and ancient snake god. It has an insatiable appetite for virgin flesh and Mary's sister Eve (Catherine Oxenburg) is on the menu. D'Ampton connects the disappearance of Eve with Lady Sylvia and, taking on his ancestor's role, heads for Thor's Cave to search for a tunnel connecting to Temple Hall. The nonsense ends in predictable fashion, with Angus emerging as the reluctant hero (wearing a kilt and playing the bagpipes), snatching Eve from the monster's jaws and slaying it with a hand grenade.

GRINDON

Thor's Cave may be the most famous cave in the Peak District but there are several others, including Ossom's Cave and Elderbush. Both have been explored and produced bones and flints from the Stone and Bronze Ages. So, Thor's Cave may have been home to one or two prehistoric beasties but in reality none of them were big white snakes. Formed over thousands of years from the combined effects of wind and rain on the soft limestone, it probably sheltered animals like giant red deer, bears or even early humans. Excavations have revealed it to be the site of a Bronze Age burial, although much of the evidence was lost by over-zealous 19th-century excavators.

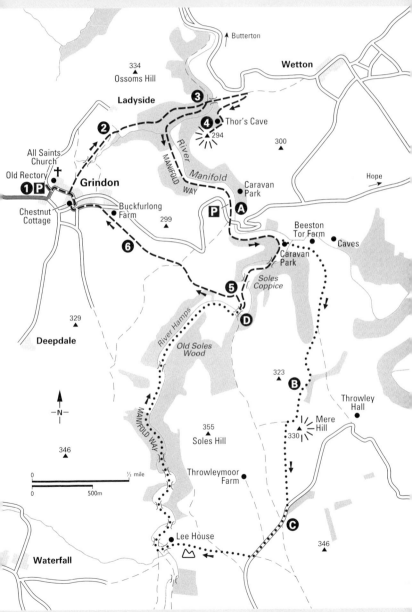

WALK 13 DIRECTIONS

❶ From the car park turn left, then right at the Old Rectory and head downhill. After 100 yds (91m) go left on to a public footpath, go through a gap stile, cross a field and head downhill on the right of two diverging paths. Cross a bridge, go through a gate then a gap stile and go downhill, keeping the stream and the wood on your right.

❷ When the wall heads left go through a gap stile on your right continuing downhill into National Trust land at Ladyside. Cross over a stile, go through a wood and then leave it via another stile. Turn right, still continuing downhill to reach a stile leading on to the Manifold Way.

❸ Cross the Manifold Way, then a bridge and take the path uphill following the signs for Thor's Cave. At the mouth of the cave turn left, continue on a track uphill, curve right before a stile and follow the path to the summit for superb views along the Manifold Valley.

❹ Retrace your steps to the Manifold Way and turn left. Continue past a car park at the caravan park and bear right on the Manifold Way and then cross two bridges. At the beginning of the third bridge cross a stile on the right and follow the path back, parallel to the road and then curving left and uphill.

❺ Go through a gate by a dried-up pond and follow the path uphill with the wall on your right. Keep straight on, through successive fields, with the church spire at Grindon ahead.

❻ Maintain your direction across fields, keeping to the left of the farm. Finally join a farm road, continue along a walled path, then turn right onto the road opposite Chestnut Cottage. Take the first left and follow this road back to the car park.

And on to Beeston Tor and Mere Hill

Extend the walk over Mere Hill,
past the impressive cliff caves of Beeston Tor.
See map and information panel for Walk 13

DISTANCE 8.5 miles (13.7km)   **MINIMUM TIME** 5hrs

ASCENT/GRADIENT 930ft (283m) ▲▲▲   **LEVEL OF DIFFICULTY** +++

WALK 14 DIRECTIONS
(Walk 13 option)

From the car park, Point **Ⓐ**, continue along the Manifold Way until you reach two paths running parallel to one another. Take the left path through the caravan park and over a bridge, following the wide gravel track round and up the side of a hill, forking right just before Beeston Tor Farm.

After 250yds (229m) of steady climbing, cross over a stile and carry on along a wide track past an abandoned barn on the left. Soon after the barn, continue through a gate, following the footpath sign to Ilam. Follow the hollow of the valley up the faint grass tracks to the corner of a dry-stone wall, just before the band of trees on the crest of the slope. (Look back over your shoulder here at the impressive cliffs and caves of Beeston Tor.) At the corner of the wall ignore the footpath sign pointing off to the left, instead continue straight up the slope with the dry-stone wall on your right to reach a prominent band of trees, Point **Ⓑ**.

Shortly after the signpost, cross a stone stile and then another stile at the top of the next field. Carry on over a false horizon and make for the summit of Mere Hill. At the summit head right along the dry-stone wall for about 100yds (91m) and then go left through a breach in the collapsed wall.

Continue straight across the field to a gate with a stone stile in the wall to the right, and carry on across the next field, aiming for the right-hand end of a copse straight ahead, Point **Ⓒ**. When you reach the road at Point **Ⓒ**, head right for 400yds (366m) until you cross a cattle grid, then cross the stile to the right just past a more obvious gravel track.

From here you can follow a footpath all the way down to the Manifold Way (it's quite steep and may be muddy after rain, so suitable footwear is essential). At the bottom of the hill, just to the left of Lee House, cross a footbridge to your left to rejoin the Manifold Way. Go right for 1.75 miles (2.8km) until you come to the stile on the left just after a bridge, Point **Ⓓ**. Continue on the original route on Walk 13.

Shopping Stoke's Potteries

Burslem provides the perfect introduction to Stoke's cultural heritage.

DISTANCE 3 miles (4.8km)	**MINIMUM TIME** 1hr 15min
ASCENT/GRADIENT 262ft (80m) ▲▲▲	**LEVEL OF DIFFICULTY** +++
PATHS Pavement and hill trail	
LANDSCAPE Streets and urban parkland	
SUGGESTED MAP OS Explorer 258 Stoke-on-Trent	
START/FINISH Grid reference: SJ 874501	
DOG FRIENDLINESS Must be on lead near roads	
PARKING Ample parking on Moorland Road by Burslem Park	
PUBLIC TOILETS On Market Place in town centre	

WALK 15 DIRECTIONS

The City of Stoke-on-Trent, known as 'the Potteries,' actually consists of six towns, each with their own sense of history, character and identity: Burslem, Fenton, Hanley, Longton, Tunstall and Stoke itself. All six owe their existence to the rich seams of coal and clay in the area which originally would have been mined at or near the surface. Both coal and clay were mined by the Romans and excavations at Trent Vale in the 1950s uncovered a pottery kiln and workshop dating from the 1st century AD. But it was in Burslem in the 16th century that the pottery revolution got underway, thanks largely to the efforts of one man, Josiah Wedgwood (see Walk 28).

In addition to being a talented craftsmen and an astute businessman, Wedgwood was also an innovator – he was the first to establish a factory for making fine pots. Until then pottery had been a cottage industry, but Wedgwood's Burslem factory set a new standard, and before long similar buildings were springing up all over Stoke. Today, Burslem still boasts the highest concentration of potteries in the city.

The walk starts at Burslem Park, an attractive patchwork of landscaped lawns and gardens opened in 1894 on the site of a former colliery. Heading into the centre of Burslem you pass Moorland Pottery, based on the historic Chelsea Works site, while further on, at Swan Square, you can visit Ceramica. Located in the old Town Hall, this award-winning heritage exhibition explores

WHILE YOU'RE THERE

Ford Green Hall, a mile (1.6km) north-east of Sneyd Hill, is a 17th-century farmhouse with a museum and period Tudor garden. It's been restored and furnished with an outstanding collection of local textiles, ceramics and furniture, while the herb garden shows how plants were once used for medicinal and even cosmetic purposes. Open Sunday to Thursday, 1–4.30pm, all year (nominal fee).

pottery-making in Burslem through the years and includes practical activities and interactive displays. It's open 10.30am–4.30pm, Tuesday to Saturday and Bank Holiday Mondays.

Heading down Nile Street you pass the site of the former Royal Doulton works, where the Staffordshire tradition of china figurines was first established. In 2005 the factory closed when production was switched overseas. A little further on is Dudson Factory Outlet, which is open Monday to Friday and Saturday morning. They now specialise in producing tableware for the catering industry, but the shop has been opened to meet a demand for reasonably priced fine quality tableware.

Next up is the Moorcroft Factory Shop, while a little further on is their Heritage Visitor Centre, complete with original bottle kiln and open daily except Sunday. Moorcroft has been making fine china for over 100 years and each piece is hand-crafted by skilled craftsmen.

WHERE TO EAT AND DRINK

Although a chain pub, the Moorland Inn offers a varied, good-value menu of traditional pub food mixed with Tex-Mex classics. There are picnic benches at the back and food is served all day long, seven days a week, year-round.

From Burslem Park head down Moorland Road past Moorland Pottery into the town centre. At the busy junction at Swan Square you can cross over at the traffic lights to visit Ceramica in the old Town Hall, otherwise turn left towards Hanley and walk down to the imposing George Hotel.

Turn left into Nile Street, past the now redeveloped site of the Royal Doulton factory on the left. Walk past Dudson Factory Outlet and Moorcroft Factory Shop and continue along the road. Just before the bridge go right onto the leafy Cobridge Greenway cycle trail, a former railway line, and follow this to the end. Turn left, then quickly left again on to Sandbach Road to reach Moorcroft Heritage Visitor Centre.

WHAT TO LOOK OUT FOR

Take time to soak up the views of Burslem and the rest of Stoke from the vantage point at the top of the Sneyd Hill. Burslem Park is a green oasis amid the urban bustle and is currently undergoing a major restoration of its gardens, paths and historic buildings with Lottery funding.

From the museum, continue along Sandbach Road and cross the traffic lights. After 400yds (366m), as the road eases round to the right, turn sharp right up the gravel path into Sneyd Hill Park and immediately take a left fork straight up the hill following the slope to the top for excellent views.

From the top of the hill start to walk back down the way you came, but soon bear left on an obvious trail contouring round the hill to the left. Follow this round and down to the cemetery and then keep going left until it rejoins the road. At the road, head right to the top of Sneyd Hill.

Turn sharp left, then left again at the final mini-roundabout, past the Moorland Inn and down Moorland Road. After about 500yds (457m) turn right on to Park Road, then immediately left to enter Burslem Park (an excellent spot for a picnic) to end the walk.

Discover Apedale's Mining Tradition

Exploring the industrial history of a wasteland that's been returned to nature.

16

DISTANCE 4.75 miles (7.7km)	**MINIMUM TIME** 2hrs
ASCENT/GRADIENT 300ft (91m) ▲▲▲	**LEVEL OF DIFFICULTY** ✦✦✦

PATHS Wide gravel tracks, roads and dirt trails, 16 stiles

LANDSCAPE Ancient woodland, farmland and hilltop

SUGGESTED MAP OS Explorer 258 Stoke-on-Trent

START/FINISH Grid reference: SJ 823484

DOG FRIENDLINESS Must be kept on lead at all times

PARKING Car park opposite Heritage Centre, gates close at dusk

PUBLIC TOILETS At Heritage Centre

Apedale Country Park, just to the west of Newcastle-under-Lyme, has a rich and varied history. The name itself has two possible meanings: one suggests that the word ape comes from the Latin *apis* meaning bee; the other is that ape is short for apple. Whichever you prefer, it seems probable that Apedale was once an ancient rural landscape, although for the last 2,000 years, it has been anything but…

Iron and Coal

Iron smelting in Apedale probably goes back at least to Roman times, if not before, but the impact on the landscape would have been negligible compared to what came later. Mining in the region is known to date back as far as the 1200s. This was made possible in the early days thanks to large deposits of coal lying at or very near the surface. Of the four main Staffordshire deposits, the Potteries Coalfield was by far the biggest, comprising an area of 100 square miles (259sq km).

The Potteries, though, were doubly blessed. Not only was there coal to be mined and sold, but there were rich seams of high quality clays that could be used to make pots. As the pottery industry developed so the demand for coal increased, and the Apedale collieries would have played a major role in meeting that demand. The arrival of the first canals in 1777, thanks partly to the vision of people like Josiah Wedgwood (see Walk 28), precipitated a boom in business throughout the region, and the emergence of the railways 60 years later proved to be another catalyst to productivity and prosperity.

A Major Centre of Production

With the Industrial Revolution well underway, iron mining and smelting enjoyed its own boom thanks to the invention of the blast furnace in the late 18th century. Apedale was a major centre of production, at one point providing employment for more than 3,000 men. Rising costs, however, sent local industry into decline by the 1920s, and when the owners lost their fortune in the Wall Street crash, it ended altogether. Coal mining in the area, however, continued until 1998, when the last deep mine was closed at Silverdale, just a mile or two to the south of Apedale.

Reclamation Work

For much of the 20th century Apedale remained a barren and desolate place but today little evidence of the area's industrial heritage remains. Nature has reclaimed the spoil heaps with luxurious ferns (see Fern Bank, on the map), and trees are recolonising the land, creating 455 acres (184ha) of woodland, meadows and pools that everyone can enjoy. Active reclamation work began in 1995 and continued efforts to improve and develop the park and its facilities are a triumph of nature over industry. Apedale Country Park is probably as green now as it's been in the last 300 years, an ancient rural landscape reborn.

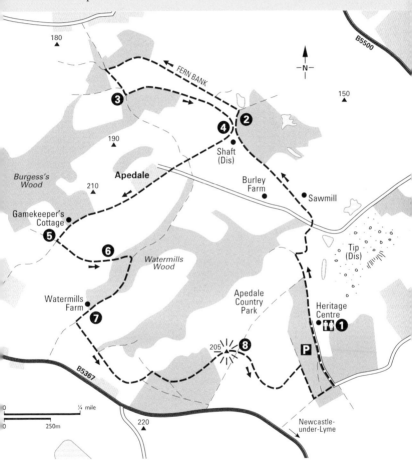

WALK 16 DIRECTIONS

❶ From the Heritage Centre in Apedale Country Park take a path to go right, through a gate. After 400yds (366m) turn right down to a corner of the park, then continue straight ahead, passing to the left of the sawmill. At a fork in the path, head right down a short hill to reach the corner of a lake.

16

❷ Ignoring the stile, turn left along the narrow path into the woods. Stay on the main path and go right before a stile to emerge into Fern Bank, containing giant, head-high ferns. Follow this path to reach a junction, with a clearing to your left. Walk through the clearing to reach the main gravel track.

❸ Turn left and continue for 600yds (549m) to a gate and the turn-off for the lake, Point ❷. About 30 paces after the gate, head right up a signed footpath along the edge of a small copse, keeping the fence to your right. At the top of this wood, 30 paces off the track to your left, is a disused mineshaft.

❹ From the top of the wood continue up the tree-lined track to the village of Apedale, a former mining community. On the right, just after the track veers to the left, is Gamekeeper's Cottage, once the site of a colliery.

❺ About 100yds (91m) beyond the cottage turn left and go over a stile by a gate. Cross the field ahead to reach another stile. Go left to yet another stile, then head right following a fence to the bottom of the hill, then skirt left to reach another stile.

❻ Cross into Watermills Wood and follow the trail to another stile, then come to a junction of two paths. Head right here and, after 10 paces, fork right again. You'll shortly come to a succession

WHERE TO EAT AND DRINK
The Heritage Centre café, conveniently situated at the start of the walk, sells a variety of drinks and snacks and is open daily between 10am and 4pm.

of stiles before continuing up to Watermills Farm.

❼ Go over a stile and continue for 100yds (91m) before following a footpath left over a series of fields and stiles to some farm buildings on your right. When the fence veers round to the left, follow it to the edge of a young plantation. At the wide gravel track, head right and at a fork go left to reach the summit and the preserved pit wheel and wagon.

WHILE YOU'RE THERE
If you have time make sure you visit the surprisingly picturesque market town of Newcastle-under-Lyme, to the south-east of Apedale. Its pedestrianised centre is a haven for shoppers, as is the market, which takes place six days a week.

❽ From the summit drop down the other side, continuing over a crossroads for a gently curving track to a T-junction. Head right here, and then take the first left down the hill. At the tarmac road head left and continue back towards the Heritage Centre.

WHAT TO LOOK OUT FOR
The highlight of the walk is undoubtedly the view from the hilltop at Point 8, where a wide circle of carved wooden posts indicates the position of various distant landmarks on the horizon, such as Mow Cop Castle, 6 miles (9.7km) to the north, and Pye Green Mast, 25 miles (40km) to the south on Cannock Chase. The scene is relatively pollution-free today, and it's hard to imagine that the view to the east was once shrouded in smog, or that 'smoky postcards' were once very popular as a souvenir of the times when plenty of smoke meant plenty of work.

Ilam and the Compleat Angler

Explore the countryside once walked by Izaak Walton,
often regarded as the 'Father of Angling'.

DISTANCE 4.75 miles (7.7km)	**MINIMUM TIME** 2hrs 30min
ASCENT/GRADIENT 607ft (185m) ▲▲▲	**LEVEL OF DIFFICULTY** ✚✚✢

PATHS Metalled roads, parkland, open hillside, meadows and forest tracks, boggy in wet weather

LANDSCAPE Parkland, woodland and hillside

SUGGESTED MAP OS Explorer OL24 White Peak

START/FINISH Grid reference: SK 131507

DOG FRIENDLINESS Keep on lead near livestock

PARKING At Ilam Hall (National Trust pay car park)

PUBLIC TOILETS At Ilam Hall

The Manifold and Dove rivers join just beyond Ilam near the Izaak Walton Hotel. Both rivers were fished by the 'Father of Angling' and the author of *The Compleat Angler*, or *The Contemplative Man's Recreation*. Since the first edition appeared in 1653 it has never been out of print.

Izaak Walton

Born in Stafford in 1593, Walton moved to London as an apprentice ironmonger, becoming a craftsman and guild member when he was 25 years old. For most of his working life he owned an ironmongers shop in Fleet Street and lived in a house in Chancery Lane. A keen angler he spent much of his spare time fishing on the Thames but it was not until retirement that he was able to devote himself to his hobby completely. 'I have laid aside business, and gone a-fishing.'

Shrewd Operator

The view we have of Walton from his book is of a genial old buffer strolling along river banks in pastoral England. But nothing could be further from the truth. Walton lived during a period of political upheaval and unrest. In 1649 he saw the execution of Charles I and left London for Staffordshire where he stayed during the Civil War. A staunch Royalist he is mentioned amongst the supporters of Charles II after the Battle of Worcester in 1651. Following the battle he visited a friend who had been imprisoned in Stafford. From this friend Walton received the King's ring, which he delivered to Colonel Blague, then a prisoner in the Tower of London. The Colonel escaped, made his way to France and returned the ring to the King. If Walton had been caught, he would have been executed. Just two years after 'the only known adventure' in his life he published his famous book.

Celebrated Work

The Compleat Angler is the story of three sportsmen, Viator, a huntsman, Auceps, a fowler and Piscator, the fisherman, walking the River Lea on

May Day debating the finer points of their chosen sport. The fifth edition in 1676 contained an addition by Walton's friend and fishing companion, Charles Cotton, who lived at Beresford Hall near Hartington. Cotton built a little fishing house on the banks of the Dove near his home, which still stands today. This 'holy shrine for all anglers' has the interlacing initials of both men and the inscription 'Piscatoribus Scarum 1674'.

Following the restoration of the monarchy and Charles II, Walton moved to Winchester as the guest of his friend George Morley, Bishop of Winchester, and lived there until he died, aged 90 on 15 December 1683. He was buried in the floor of the Chapel of St John the Evangelist and the Fisherman Apostles.

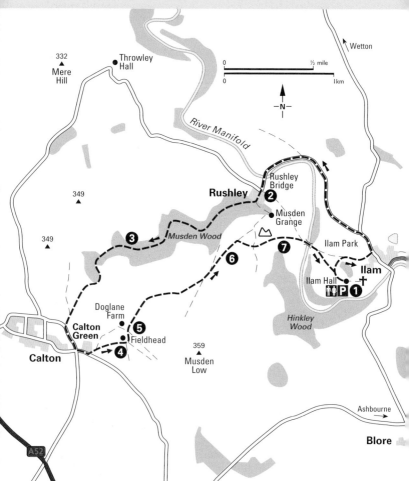

WALK 17 DIRECTIONS

❶ Leave the car park from the corner (pedestrian exit), turn right through a gate and follow the track through the park. Cross a stile and turn left on to the road out of Ilam village. Go uphill, turn left at Park Cottage on to the Castern to Throwley road. At a Y-junction go left, following the road across Rushley Bridge.

2 Go through Rushley Farm and then turn right, through a gate, on to the public footpath. Cross a ladder stile, walk along the side of a fence and then cross a gate on the left. Continue ahead following the waymarked path beside a stone wall and a fence, walking along the valley bottom.

3 Go over a series of stiles and at the final one, turn left onto the road. At the crossroads turn left towards Ashbourne. Go left through a gap stile at the next public footpath sign and cross the field. Cross a stile, go through another field to a stile to the left of a farm, then head diagonally left across the next field.

4 Cross the wall by stone steps, then head diagonally right to a gap stile to the right of some buildings. Continue on this line to another stile in the hedge to the right of Fieldhead farm and turn left on to the drive. Follow this round the boundary of the farm and go over a stile on the right by a metal gate.

5 Follow the field-edge path uphill. Cross a stile, cross the field to where two walls meet at a corner and follow the wall to the right. Join a farm road, pass a derelict farmstead, then turn diagonally right across a field and through a gap stile in the wall at the far corner.

6 Follow the direction pointer past two marker stones to the next public footpath sign and go right. Follow the wall on your right, go through a gap, follow the waymarker downhill.

7 Go across two fields, a stile and then a bridge and into Ilam Park. Turn right and at the stile fork left, uphill, on a broad track that crosses the grounds back to the car park.

The Limestone of Caldonlow

*The geology of this region provides
a backdrop to a spectacular walk.*

18

> **DISTANCE** 6 miles (9.7km) **MINIMUM TIME** 2hrs 30min
>
> **ASCENT/GRADIENT** 480ft (146m) ▲▲ **LEVEL OF DIFFICULTY** ✦✦✦
>
> **PATHS** Field and woodland paths, can be muddy, 19 stiles
>
> **LANDSCAPE** Farmland, quarry and hilltop
>
> **SUGGESTED MAP** OS Explorer 259 Derby; OL24 White Peak (Walk 19)
>
> **START/FINISH** Grid reference: SK 086494 on Explorer 259
>
> **DOG FRIENDLINESS** Must be kept on lead near livestock
>
> **PARKING** Roadside parking at start point near cement works
>
> **PUBLIC TOILETS** None en route (nearest at Waterhouses car park
> by cycle hire centre)

The story of Caldonlow begins around 350 million years ago during the Carboniferous period. Thanks to the whims of continental drift the North Staffordshire moorlands and the Peak District of Derbyshire were much further south than they are today and the region was covered by a shallow tropical sea. Over millions of years, a layer of shells and coral slowly built up on the seabed, both formed from the calcium carbonate secretions of a variety of marine animals.

The Creation of Limestone

As there was little current to disturb these deposits, this layer was slowly compacted by additional layers of sediment, again over millions of years, to create limestone. If you remember your school chemistry, you'll know that chalk, marble and limestone are all calcium carbonate, each made under different conditions. Limestone is in fact almost pure calcium carbonate and as a result is very light in colour (hence the name White Peak, as opposed to the gritstone areas of the Dark Peak further north).

Quarries

In places like the White Peak, subsequent weathering, erosion and the ice age, scoured away the softer topsoil leaving the limestone outcrops at or near the surface, which could then be readily quarried. And this is precisely what happened at Caldonlow Quarry, which at the height of the Industrial Revolution was yielding some 6,000 tons a week. The valuable limestone was transported on a tramway to the terminus of the Caldon Canal at Froghall, 3 miles (4.8km) to the west (see Walk 21), and from there it was taken by barge to Stoke, Macclesfield and other canal-fed towns across the Midlands.

Then, as now, limestone had a great many uses. High-quality stone was used directly for building, while aggregate (crushed stone) was used for making roads. When calcium carbonate is heated, it leaves a deposit of calcium oxide or quicklime. Quicklime is even more useful than limestone.

CALDONLOW

As a fertiliser it improves crop yields by reducing the acidity of soil, and it also reacts with the main impurities in iron ore to make iron and calcium silicate (or slag), which floats on top of the molten iron and is removed for use in road building.

A Site of Special Scientific Interest

At Froghall, the limestone was fired in massive kilns to produce quicklime to be shipped direct to customers. Today, the wharf and the lime kilns are long abandoned and the quarry at Caldonlow is much quieter than it was 150 years ago. It's now a designated geological Site of Special Scientific Interest and is dominated by the massive cement works at the start of the walk. It won't come as a surprise to learn that cement is a mixture of clay and quicklime.

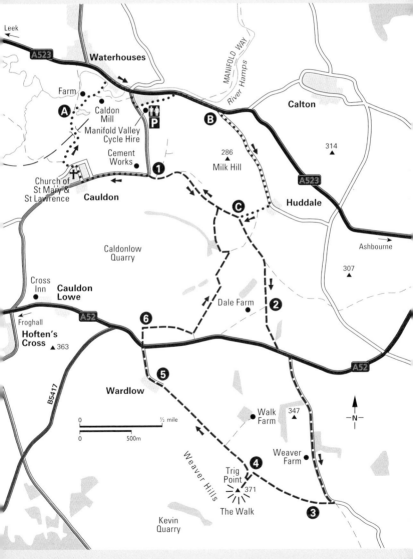

WALK 18 DIRECTIONS

❶ From the road corner head east along the gravel track, walking away from Cauldon. At the first corner go straight on for a track up a small valley. Pass a barn on your right, go through a slot or swing gate and then take the right fork along a wide dirt track. Go through the second gate ahead of you and after 25 paces go right, through an overgrown area, for a small stile into a wide, sloping field. Carry on straight up the hill.

❷ At the top right-hand corner of the field, go through a gate and straight across the next field to a gap in the wall ahead. After the gap, head for the bottom left-hand corner of the next field and cross a stile on to the A52. Bear left for 100yds (91m), then turn right along the narrow metalled road past Weaver Farm. As the road veers to the left there are two footpath signs on the right: at the first of these go back on yourself, up the hill towards a gate in the dry-stone wall.

❸ After crossing the stile here keep following the dry-stone wall to your right and at the next gate

continue in the same direction, with the wall to your left. At the end of this wall bear slightly right to join another wall on the right and follow it to the gate.

❹ Before crossing the dry-stone wall ahead of you, go left for 100yds (91m) and then right over a stile, before making straight for the trig point. From the trig point retrace your steps to the stile, but instead of crossing it, head left across the field, making for the dry-stone wall at the bottom. Follow this wall all the way to Wardlow.

❺ Continue as far as the A52 and go straight across, following a public footpath sign. Continue over the thistly plateau of this field to a stile.

❻ Turn right, go over another stile and along a waymarked route through the narrow belt of trees. At the far end go ahead along the right edge of the field. Follow it all the way round to cross the stile in the far left corner. Turn right and go down the field edge to a stile. Go left for 100yds (91m) and then right along a trail through a narrow valley. At the bottom of the valley rejoin the main track to return to the start point.

Waterhouses and the Manifold Way

If you have the time, extend the walk to Waterhouses, and take in the start of the Manifold Way.
See map and information panel for Walk 18

19

DISTANCE 9 miles (14.5km)   **MINIMUM TIME** 3hrs 45min
ASCENT/GRADIENT 751ft (229m) ▲▲▲   **LEVEL OF DIFFICULTY** +++

WALK 19 DIRECTIONS (Walk 18 option)

From Point **1**, at the corner of the road, head west towards Cauldon village, up a gentle slope passing the cement works on your right. Take the second right into the village (look out for an old water fountain with its whimsical poem carved into the stone just before the turning) and then continue up the hill as far as the Church of St Mary and St Lawrence. Turn left just after the church and then, after 100yds (91m), turn right along a wide gravel track. After another 100yds (91m), head right at a sharp left bend and follow the path round until it runs beside an old railway embankment dropping away to the left. Head left, over an overgrown bridge, and drop down the far side of the embankment to reach a wide gravel track, Point **A**.

Follow the small lake around to the left. Beyond a stile by a wide gate turn right on to another track and follow the waymarkers to the left to find an overgrown path down to a farmyard. Keep to the right of the farm buildings for a driveway to Caldon Mill and then left to reach the A523. Go right for 250yds (229m) through this quiet village and then turn right (shortly going under a disused

railway bridge) and then first left to Manifold Valley Cycle Hire and the start of the Manifold Way (see Walk 8) – the building is a part of the old station. Follow the cycle track until it drops down to reach the A523. Now turn right and walk along the pavement for 650 yards (594m).

At Point **B** turn right along this quiet road and follow it as far as Huddale. Turn right here along a track to regain the main route at Point **C**. Retrace your steps to the start.

WHAT TO LOOK OUT FOR

The River Hamps, which runs through Waterhouses alongside the A523, is often seen (or, more precisely, not seen) to be flowing underground. This is because the limestone bedrock is porous and in many places, particularly when the water levels are low, the river can disappear into so-called swallow holes to flow through underground channels, exposing the dry river bed of water-smoothed limestone.

Conservation at Consall

A canal and woodland walk looking at man's impact on the area.

20

DISTANCE 3.5 miles (5.7km)	**MINIMUM TIME** 1hr 30min
ASCENT/GRADIENT 360ft (110m) ▲▲▲	**LEVEL OF DIFFICULTY** ✦✦✦
PATHS Gravel tracks, tow paths and roads, can be muddy, 13 stiles	
LANDSCAPE Canal, meadow and woodland	
SUGGESTED MAP OS Explorers 258 Stoke-on-Trent; 259 Derby	
START/FINISH Grid reference: SJ 944483 on Explorer 258	
DOG FRIENDLINESS Must be kept on lead	
PARKING Consall Nature Park visitor centre	
PUBLIC TOILETS At visitor centre	

WALK 20 DIRECTIONS

Consall Nature Park, like Dimmings Dale near Alton (see Walk 23), is a part of the Churnet Valley and has a long industrial history. Iron working is known to have taken place here as early as the 13th century, when vast tracts of woodland were felled to provide charcoal for smelting. Later, towards the end of the 18th century, the place was mined for ironstone, and the arrival of the Caldon Canal (see Walk 21) and the Churnet Valley Railway meant it was once again stripped of trees to make way for progress. At its peak, 1,500 men worked here, filling 30 barges a day with iron ore.

Today, this region has been largely reclaimed by nature, but many landmarks remain. The railway, for example, was built in 1849 to link Manchester and Macclesfield with the rest of the Midlands, transporting iron ore, coal and limestone all over the district. Although it stopped operating commercially in the 1960s, it

has been given a new lease of life as a tourist attraction, and the once-derelict Consall Station has been lovingly restored. Before the arrival of the railway, the Caldon Canal served a similar purpose, and there are still giant lime kilns where the canal and the river meet. These kilns were used to burn limestone from the vast Caldonlow quarries near by to produce quicklime, which could then be used in fertiliser or in mortar (see Walk 18).

Even the Black Lion pub was built in the early 1800s specially to serve the men who lived and worked in the area. To this day it's still not accessible by road. Back

WHAT TO LOOK OUT FOR

At the pond by the visitor centre, look out for resident water voles. They're not the most outgoing of animals and their burrow – a nest made of rushes and grass – is often below the surface. You should be able to see signs of their existence, from tracks in the mud to the nibbled tops of pond plants.

then, it could be reached only by a cart track, by the steep steps running up beside the kilns, by canal and, later, by rail.

At the top of the steps beside the kilns are the remnants of spoil heaps, but the further you go from the river, the harder it is to find evidence of the damage done in the name of progress. In 1994 the Consall Nature Park was designated as a Site of Special Scientific Interest, as the largest area of semi-natural woodland in Staffordshire. Today, this region is dominated by birch trees since these are often the first to recover after deforestation. There are no large trees since these were felled when the original forest was cleared for charcoal, mining and railways, although there are signs that oak trees may be starting to establish themselves, protected in their youth by the silver birches.

> ### WHILE YOU'RE THERE
> Spend some time in Consall Nature Park Visitor Centre: it has a touch table, interactive displays, and information on both the industrial and natural history of the area. It also sells cold drinks and snacks.

From the car park head to the left of the visitor centre to join a road. Go right and, at the far bottom of the road, bear diagonally right over a field to cross a footbridge. Follow the path right and then left to reach the corner of a bridge across a railway. Cross the bridge and go right down a set of steps, then right along the tow path.

Soon after you pass Consall Station on your left, walk under the railway opposite The Black Lion pub and cross the canal and then the river. Just to the left of the lime kiln go up 202 steep steps

and, at the top, walk right, along a grass track. At the brow of the hill follow the path to a gate and two little mounds. After picking your way through these mounds, cross the stile in the corner of the field and, after 30 paces, walk right through the gate. Head diagonally left across this field to cross a stile and continue on the track. At the metalled road go right.

> ### WHERE TO EAT AND DRINK
> The Black Lion, in the heart of the Churnet Valley, is a great place for a pie and pint. It does the usual bar snacks and has an extensive restaurant menu. Food is served daily in summer

After 600yds (549m) reach a black-and-white timbered farmhouse on your right in the village of Consall. Just after a T-junction (signposted to Leek) go left across a farmyard following a signed public footpath. Cross a stile, continue along the wide track to another stile, then following a line of trees just to your left-hand side. Carry on through a series of stiles to the corner of a wood.

In the wood carry straight on, ignoring the trail to your left. When the path you're on bears left, follow it to cross a stile back into Consall Nature Park. Go straight down the hill, again ignoring a path to the left. At the bottom, head left along the wider track. When this joins an even wider grassy track, bear right and continue straight on, ignoring paths to the left and right.

By a water outpipe, follow the track round to the right. Then go left at the fork, pass a fishing lake to your right and return to the visitor centre.

Overleaf: A bridge over the Caldon Canal (Walk 20)

21

Staffordshire's Steepest Railway

A circular walk exploring the problems encountered by engineers at Froghall's well-preserved wharf.

DISTANCE 4.5 miles (7.2km)	**MINIMUM TIME** 2hrs
ASCENT/GRADIENT 650ft (198m) ▲▲▲	**LEVEL OF DIFFICULTY** +++

PATHS Grass paths and dirt tracks may be muddy and slippery in very wet weather; 13 stiles

LANDSCAPE Forest and farmland

SUGGESTED MAP OS Explorer 259 Derby

START/FINISH Grid reference: SK 027477

DOG FRIENDLINESS Keep on lead near livestock

PARKING Froghall Wharf car park

PUBLIC TOILETS At Froghall Wharf picnic site

These days Froghall Wharf is a very pleasant and secluded picnic site at the heart of North Staffordshire's Churnet Valley but this hasn't always been the case. In 1777 the Caldon Canal from Stoke-on-Trent to Froghall was completed by engineering whizz James Brindley (see Walk 10). Froghall was chosen as the site for the eastern terminus of the canal because of its proximity to the limestone quarries situated at Caldonlow, just 3 miles (4.8km) to the east.

Transporting Limestone

In theory, the limestone could have been taken from the quarry to Froghall on a basic tramway and then loaded on to barges bound for Stoke-on-Trent. In practice however, the quarries were some 680ft (207m) higher than the canal, which meant building the tramway was almost as difficult as building the canal. The first version, with rails of wood topped by an iron strip, was built in 1778, but soon proved to be inadequate. A replacement, completed in 1785, fared little better. A few years later, though, a third line was built and this was made more efficient by an ingenious device called a brake drum. Full wagons at the top of the incline were attached to empty wagons at the bottom via a large wooden drum; when these loaded wagons were rolled to the bottom, the empty wagons were pulled to the top, letting gravity do all the hard work.

At The Wharf

By the start of the 19th century, the tramway was delivering thousands of tons of limestone a week to Froghall Wharf. In the 1840s a fourth line was built, which followed a virtually straight line to the quarry, and this line remained in use right up until 1920. When the limestone reached the wharf it was either loaded directly onto barges to be taken to Stoke for use in construction or it was fed into the tops of the enormous lime kilns that can still be seen at the wharf today. Layers of coal were added and then the mixture was fired to reduce the limestone to quicklime. This was then collected at the bottom and taken to nearby farms for use as a fertiliser; quicklime was also used in mortar and as an ingredient in smelting iron from iron ore (see Walk 18).

Special Site

Today, Froghall Wharf has been designated a Site of Special Scientific Interest (SSSI), thanks to its flower meadows and large areas of woodland, which support 50 species of birds, plus many more species of insects dependent on over-mature trees.

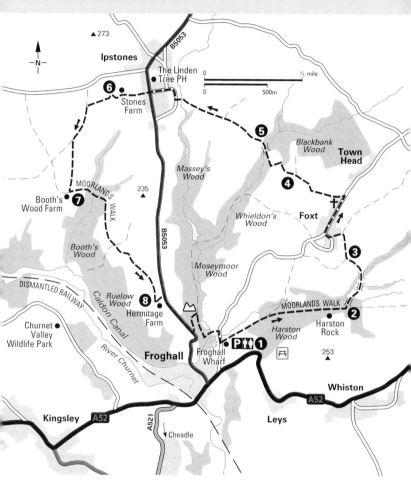

WALK 21 DIRECTIONS

1 From the car park go up a short ramp and along the gravel track. At the fork head right and, just after Harston Rock, go left down a trail signed 'Moorlands Walk'. At the bottom cross a footbridge.

2 Shortly after the footbridge, cross a stile and the bottom of a field. Once back in the woods again, cross another footbridge and go through a narrow stone slot. Continue across a field to a stile and another footbridge. Cross another stile and follow a dry-stone wall up the hill.

3 At the top bear right and continue round, following the curve of the wall. After a slot, go down a gravel track to a surfaced road and then head right to the wide fork. Go right through Foxt and after the church go hard left down the rough road.

4 Just before a private drive go left and then across a stile on the right, following the path along a fence. After crossing the stile continue through the wood to a small stream. Cross and shortly after go through a kissing gate and follow the path to a farm road.

5 Turn right to Ipstones. At the end, follow the footpath round to the left and then immediately up stone steps to the road. Follow the road right and then round to the left and, at the next corner, continue between the houses and along a road. At the main road go right then left along the footpath (signed) to Stones Farm.

6 Bear slightly to the left of the farm and, just past it, go through a gate on your right and then continue left along the track. Go through a gate and carry on to a gap in the wall ahead. In the next field cross diagonally left to a gap

in a hedge. Continue down the field to cross a stile in the far right corner. Keep on down the left-hand edge of this field to a track to Booth's Wood Farm (aim for the near corner of the buildings).

7 Cross a stile and head left following the Moorlands Walk into Booth's Wood and follow a stepped footpath down to a footbridge. At the top of the wood go through the gate and across the field to the corner of a dry-stone wall. Follow this wall and track to reach Hermitage Farm.

8 Go right on the main road and, after 400yds (366m), follow the footpath sign into the woods on the left. Follow this steep path down to a T-junction, then turn right to the canal. At the canal turn left towards the bridge, then cross it to reach the car park.

Ellastone and its Fictional Past

*Discover the area that was the source of inspiration
for an infamous author and a famous composer.*

22

DISTANCE 4 miles (6.4km)	**MINIMUM TIME** 1hr 30min
ASCENT/GRADIENT 360ft (110m) ▲▲▲	**LEVEL OF DIFFICULTY** +++
PATHS Gravel tracks, roads and grass trails, 11 stiles	
LANDSCAPE Farmland	
SUGGESTED MAP OS Explorer 259 Derby	
START/FINISH Grid reference: SK 118426	
DOG FRIENDLINESS Must be kept on lead	
PARKING Ample parking along village roads	
PUBLIC TOILETS None en route	

Ellastone, near the Derbyshire border to the south-west of Ashbourne, is known for its literary and its musical associations, both of which involve people named George – or so it would seem. The first is George Eliot, author of – among others – *Silas Marner* (1861) and *Middlemarch* (1871). Eliot's first novel *Adam Bede* is based on the village of Ellastone; in the book it is referred to as Hayslope, while Staffordshire is named Loamshire. When it was first published in 1859, by a completely unknown author, a number of impostors tried to claim authorship of the book. Only then was it revealed that George Elliot was a pen name for Marian Evans, who wrote for the prestigious *Westminster Review*.

A Victorian Scandal

The scandal that broke when it was discovered that George Eliot was a woman was exacerbated by the fact that she was also having an extra-marital affair with George Henry Lewis, her editor. Unable to divorce his faithless wife, George Henry entered into a common-law marriage with George Eliot. Polite Victorian society was far too conservative for such sordid behaviour, and the author was ostracised by her family and friends. This rejection became one of the themes of her next novel, *The Mill on the Floss*, published in 1860.

Reflecting the Real World

As for *Adam Bede*, its success then, as now, lay in Eliot's ability to reflect everyday life in her characters and the worlds they inhabited. Shunning the romanticism prevalent in the first half of the 19th century she was one of the first writers to insist on realism, believing that novels should reflect not only the real world, but also some underlying moral purpose above and beyond the entertainment to be had from a good read. In *Adam Bede*, the hero is thought to have been based heavily on Marian's own father, and in amongst a tragic love story – interlaced with rich descriptions of rural life – lies the novel's central theme, that selflessness is the secret of happiness.

A Great Composer

The second George to find inspiration in Ellastone was George Frideric Handel (1685–1759), who was later described by Beethoven as the 'the greatest composer who ever lived'. Handel's most famous work is arguably *The Messiah*, which he composed in a furious 24 days while staying with friends at Calwich Abbey in 1741 (Calwich Abbey is passed in the early stages of the walk). *The Messiah* was first performed, in aid of charity, in Dublin a year later, where it was met with rapturous applause. Some years later, King George II was so moved on hearing the Hallelujah Chorus that he rose to his feet; the audience duly followed his example and the tradition remains today, even in the absence of royalty.

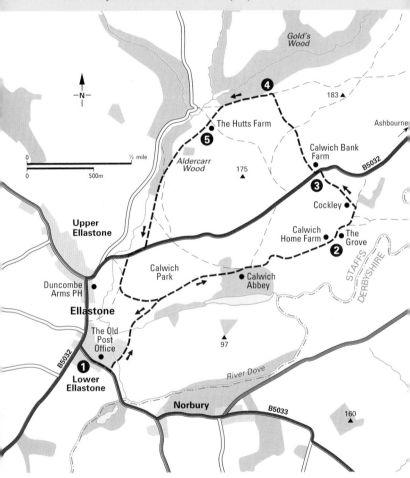

WALK 22 DIRECTIONS

❶ From the former post office, opposite the red post box, go left and then take the first left down an obvious gravel track. Keep going straight to Calwich Abbey.

Follow the track left of the abbey and along the metalled road as far as Calwich Home Farm.

❷ Pass the farm and follow the track round to the left of The Grove and through a gate. At the fork follow the yellow footpath arrows to your left and, after 50yds (46m), veer left off the track up a short hill to a stile in front of Cockley farm. Cross the stile and head just to the right of Cockley, following a dirt and grass track all the way to the B5032.

3 At the road go left and then first right, through Calwich Bank Farm and up a gravel track. When the track bears round to the right, keep going straight into a field, making for a gap in the hedge at the top right-hand corner. Shortly after this gap, go through a gate on the right and then follow the hedge left, down the field.

4 At the bottom follow the hedge round to the left and cut diagonally right across the field to a stile. After crossing the stile, skirt round the top of the wood to another stile and continue as far as The Hutts Farm. After a stile take the gravel track up the hill to a gate into the farmyard and head straight on to another stile into a field.

5 Continue straight across, making for the corner of Aldercarr Wood. Keep going to the stile in the bottom right-hand corner of

22

the field and carry on along the right-hand edge of the next field. At the far end cross another stile and continue straight on (not diagonally left) to the B5032. Turn right along the road and, after 100yds (91m), take the path to the left. Head diagonally right across the field to a double stile and then left round the bottom of a small mound with trees. Keep going as far as the junction of the two bridleways, between Point **1** and Point **2**, and from here retrace your steps back to the post office.

The Quieter Side of Alton

A tranquil walk from the village made famous by its theme park.

23

> **DISTANCE** 5 miles (8km) **MINIMUM TIME** 1hr 45min
>
> **ASCENT/GRADIENT** 361ft (110m) ▲▲▲ **LEVEL OF DIFFICULTY** ✦✦✦
>
> **PATHS** Roads, gravel tracks and dirt trails
>
> **LANDSCAPE** Forest and farmland
>
> **SUGGESTED MAP** OS Explorer 259 Derby
>
> **START/FINISH** Grid reference: SK 072423
>
> **DOG FRIENDLINESS** Must be kept on lead near livestock
>
> **PARKING** Parking on Alton village roads
>
> **PUBLIC TOILETS** None en route

For its size, the village of Alton has more than its fair share of history, not to mention a name that's practically synonymous with stomach-churning, roller-coaster rides. The first recorded settlement in the area was an Iron Age fort on Bunbury Hill – the site of the present day Alton Towers – built before 1000 BC. In the 8th century AD it became a fortress for the Saxon king Coelred and in the 12th century it was given to a soldier by the name of Bertram de Verdun, as a thanks for the part he played in the crusades.

A Conspicuous Castle

In 1176 de Verdun built a castle high above Churnet Valley, on the opposite side to the original fort. The castle remains are at the start of the walk but they're on the site of a children's centre, so you can only glimpse the ruined tower and walls. A sheer cliff lies below the north side, and on the east and south sides is a deep ditch. The lower parts of a wall remain, as does most of a rectangular tower and the base of a round tower. The castle is thought to have been in a state of neglect at the time of Verdun's death, and subsequent centuries did little to stop the rot. It was held for King Charles in the Civil War but later dismantled by Parliament to stop it being used by Royalists.

Opposite the castle is the present-day Catholic Youth Centre, begun in 1847 to a design by A W Pugin, who was partly responsible for the Houses of Parliament. Pugin was at the vanguard of the Gothic revival, when every landowner wanted a mock castle on his land, hence the battlemented cornices. Originally a private home, it was used as a boarding school from 1919 until 1989; and has been a youth centre since 1995.

While Pugin was rebuilding the estate, successive generations of Talbots began to rebuild the landscape, especially the area of Dimmings Dale to the west of Alton. Ore smelting had flourished in the valley for 150 years but by 1850 the industry was gone. Hillsides had been stripped of trees to fire smelting furnaces, spoil heaps littered the valley and the stream had been dammed to provide water to operate the smelting mill. Today, thanks to the Talbot family, the forest has been restored and the spoil heaps are gone, but the lakes and the original mill still remain as part of a peaceful forest walk.

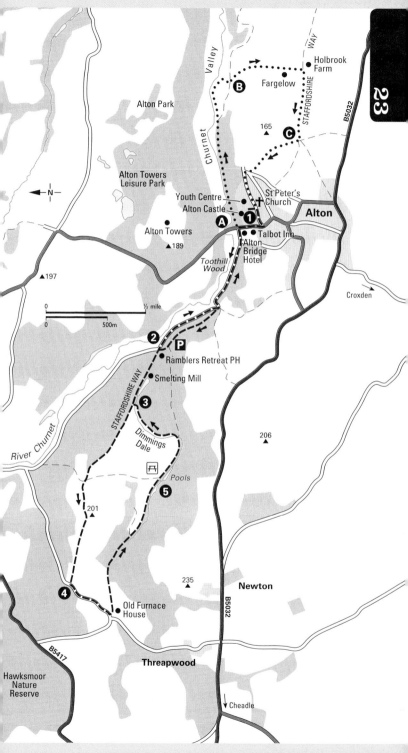

WALK 23 DIRECTIONS

❶ At the castle gate, head straight down the track to the right of St Peter's Church. At the main road, head right, down the hill to the river and the Alton Bridge Hotel. Head left along a metalled road, past the hotel, going straight ahead where the road goes round to the left, along the base of Toothill Wood. Just after the road goes round an obvious hairpin bend, follow a wide track into the woods on the left, shown by a public bridleway sign. After 400yds (366m) go right off the track down a less obvious trail which will bring you out at Dimmings Dale car park and the Ramblers Retreat pub.

WHILE YOU'RE THERE

The Hawksmoor Nature Reserve has been in existence since 1927. It was originally the site of an iron-smelting furnace and at Gibridding you can still see the remains of an inclined plane which was once a tramway used for hauling coal from the extensive mines at Cheadle to the Froghall to Uttoxeter canal. The wood is a haven for insects and birds, including spotted fly-catchers in summer and occasional buzzards in the winter.

❷ Go through the car park to the right of the pub and then continue straight on following signs for the Staffordshire Way. Pass the smelting mill and lake on your left, and continue straight on at the end of the lake, staying to the right of the impressive stone house.

❸ When you climb up to a path junction amid the open woods, go straight over, following more Staffordshire Way signs, and still ascending. At the top of the hill go right along the metalled road, over

WHERE TO EAT AND DRINK

The Ramblers Retreat is in a very secluded spot in the heart of the Churnet Valley, just a few minutes' walk from Dimmings Dale. The food, ranging from cakes and snacks right through to three-course meals, is invariably excellent. Closed Mondays except bank holidays, the pub is open 10am–5pm Tues-Sun year-round.

a cattle grid and follow this road all the way to a T-junction.

❹ Go left at the junction and, after 400yds (366m), go left again just before Old Furnace House. When you get to a fork in the track, head right, close to the stream and past a series of pools, until you get to a picnic table and a causeway between two pools.

❺ Continue to the left of the stream after the final pool, staying on the left at the first wooden footbridge. When you get to a dry-stone wall barring the way straight ahead, go right over a wooden footbridge and continue to follow the river left. This path will shortly bring you back to the smelting mill and the Ramblers Retreat. From there head along the road back to the hotel and then retrace your steps back to St Peter's Church.

WHAT TO LOOK OUT FOR

The old smelting mill is now a private residence and it's hard to see any detail, but the original waterwheel is still there and you can't miss the necklace of pools that stretches up the valley. The mill was built in 1741 and was used for forging lead ore. After the decline of the smelting industry near the end of the century, it was converted to a corn mill, its 20ft (6m) wheel driving three pairs of grinding stones.

The Churnet Valley

*Extend the walk with a loop that
overlooks abundant woodland.*
See map and information panel for Walk 23

24

DISTANCE *7 miles (11.3km)* **MINIMUM TIME** *2hrs 45min*
ASCENT/GRADIENT *233ft (71m)* ▲▲▲ **LEVEL OF DIFFICULTY** +++

WALK 24 DIRECTIONS
(Walk 23 options)

From the hotel car park go right, Point **Ⓐ**, across the main road, and follow a wide gravel track along the Churnet Valley. After 0.5 mile (800m), follow a Countryside Care footpath sign off the main track to the left just before a private drive. Take the path down to the river and then follow the river around to the right. Just before the river bears left again, head right, straight up the bank to a stile across the track, Point **Ⓑ**.

After the stile, cross the track and go straight up the steep slope ahead, through a gap in the rocky outcrop. Near the top of this short slope, bear slightly left to a small stile and then head diagonally left across the field to its top left corner. Cross over the stile before heading right and then go straight up the field, keeping a hedge just to your right. At the top of this field go right through the gate and then left over a stile hidden in the hedge at the far end of the gate. After this stile, continue up the hedge as far as the ruins of Fargelow farm. Carry on to the left of this building to a gate at Holbrook Farm.

Through the gate, head right along a wide, grassy track (it's hard-going initially, but the tussocks soon give way to stone and then gravel). After 600yds (549m), just before you get to a building, you reach two stiles, one to the left and one right, Point **Ⓒ**. Follow the Staffordshire Way signpost right into a field, then skirt around the right-hand edge. At the top of this field go straight across the stile and, at the end of this field, follow it round to the left for 20 paces to get to the well-hidden stile. After the stile, head diagonally left across the field to a pair of stiles in the corner of the field.

At the road head right and, when you get to the big stone barn straight head, turn left, following the road down to Alton Castle and St Peter's Church.

WHILE YOU'RE THERE
Founded at the end of the 12th century, Croxden Abbey was one of the last Cistercian abbeys to be built in England, and its architecture is more elaborate than earlier monasteries built by this strict order. The east end was unusually ornate, consisting of five chapels radiating from an ambulatory, of which only fragments now remain. Today, the massive west front dominates the ruins, with rich mouldings around the middle doorway and three slender windows.

Trentham's Capable Gardens

Enjoying the lasting legacy of England's greatest landscape gardener.

25

DISTANCE 3.75 miles (6km)   **MINIMUM TIME** 1hr 30min

ASCENT/GRADIENT 311ft (95m) ▲▲▲   **LEVEL OF DIFFICULTY** +++

PATHS Wide gravel trail and dirt tracks

LANDSCAPE Lakeshore and woodland

SUGGESTED MAP OS Explorer 258 Stoke-on-Trent

START/FINISH Grid reference: SJ 868406

DOG FRIENDLINESS Must be kept on lead at all times

PARKING Large car park at main entrance to Trentham Estate

PUBLIC TOILETS Trentham Estate 'Village' and by Lakeside Café

WALK 25 DIRECTIONS

Trentham's long history dates back to Saxon times when Werburgh, daughter of pagan King Wulfere (AD 657–676), established a nunnery here (see Walk 31), and both Saxon and Danish foundations have been found at the site of St Mary's Church.

Successive houses were built here and, in 1834, Trentham Hall was remodelled by Sir Charles Barry who went on to design the Houses of Parliament with renowned architect Augustus Pugin (see Walk 23). The hall was demolished in 1911 and little remains of the elegant buildings. Today the estate is famous for its gardens.

The shape and extent of the park had largely been established by the 16th century, extending as far as the present-day M6, with long, straight, rides criss-crossing King's Wood. This was, after all, the time of the Renaissance, when artists and builders were re-learning the lessons of the Greeks and Romans and using them to their

own ends. In France, great palace gardens, like those at Versailles, were constructed based on simple geometric shapes and straight lines. Characteristic of this style were arrow-straight drives radiating out from the main stately pile, and it wasn't long before such ideas became all the rage in England, albeit in a slightly less rigid way. But before long, a backlash was brewing.

Lancelot 'Capability' Brown (the nickname came from his habit of telling clients that their gardens had 'great capabilities') was the leading protagonist of what would later become known as the serpentine style. Instead of accepting the idea that garden design should reflect the laws and science of nature, he suggested that it should reflect nature itself –

WHERE TO EAT AND DRINK

There are plenty of outlets at 'The Village' at the start, but the Lakeside Café at the southern end of the lake is ideally placed for drinks and light refreshments.

where, Brown asked, were straight lines to be found in the wild? For Brown, a simple curve was the epitome of all things good and noble in a landscape, designed in such a way as to make them appear natural. In this respect, he and his contemporaries were also heavily influenced by the landscapes of late Renaissance painters, with their classical buildings and carefully contrived vistas based on Greek and Roman poetry.

WHILE YOU'RE THERE

Tittensor Chase, a few miles to the south of Trentham Gardens, is another great place for walking. It's also the site of Bury Bank Fort, a pre-Roman, Iron-Age earthwork. The raised mound at the south end is believed to be the grave of King Wulfere of Mercia (AD 657–676), see Walk 31.

The result was a quest for the 'ideal' landscape, and Brown's own ideal soon proved to be phenomenally popular. In all he was involved in well over 150 gardens, among them those at Trentham. Here, he softened the formal planning of the existing estate with more serpentine rides, and dammed the Trent to create a lake that looks natural. Originally, the area in front of the hall would have been filled with graceful, sweeping lawns, merging almost imperceptibly with the 'untamed' wilderness beyond.

The formal gardens that you can see at Trentham today were laid out by Sir Charles Barry in 1839. After years of neglect, the garden and its buildings have been renovated by award-winning garden designers, who have given the gardens a more contemporary feel by extensive replanting, including 70,000 new plants and over 100,000 spring-flowering bulbs. In addition, the wider site now includes a new shopping 'village', garden centre and hotel.

Next to the entrance to the Italian Gardens in 'The Village' is a path signposted 'Lakeside & Woodland Walks'. Follow this all the way to the end of the lake.

With the lake directly behind you, walk away from the Lakeside Café and Boathouse and go right, through the car park for the 'Trentham Active' attractions. After the gate, turn left for a steep path up to the Monument.

Retrace your steps and at the café turn left to resume the Lakeside Walk. Stay on this waymarked path through woodland and past the Deer Lawn, a fenced sanctuary for the resident fallow deer. When you eventually come to a high fence across the path go through the gate and turn right on the waymarked Park Walk. Continue down beside the fence on the public footpath.

Go through a kissing gate, over a stone bridge and turn right on to a surfaced drive. Go right again, over another bridge, and ahead through gateposts following signs for the 'Lakeside & Park Walks' past old buildings. After another bridge swing right to reach the Garden Centre and beyond that 'The Village' and the start of the walk.

WHAT TO LOOK OUT FOR

The monument on Tittensor Hill was erected in 1834 in memory of George Granville, 1st Duke of Sutherland. The second statue worth noting is the bronze of Perseus and Medusa in 1847. Together, these statues defined the main axis of the estate and recent tree clearance has helped re-establish this important vista with views over the lake towards the Italian Gardens.

The Battle of Boreheath

A gentle walk around one of the bloodiest battlegrounds on English soil.

> **DISTANCE** 5.5 miles (8.8km)   **MINIMUM TIME** 2hrs
>
> **ASCENT/GRADIENT** 240ft (73m) ▲▲▲   **LEVEL OF DIFFICULTY** ✦✦✦
>
> **PATHS** Gravel tracks, roads and grass trails, 11 stiles
>
> **LANDSCAPE** Woodland and farmland
>
> **SUGGESTED MAP** OS Explorer 243 Market Drayton
>
> **START/FINISH** Grid reference: SJ 738359
>
> **DOG FRIENDLINESS** Keep on lead near livestock
>
> **PARKING** Ample parking in Loggerheads village
>
> **PUBLIC TOILETS** None en route

Loggerhead, meaning 'blockhead' or 'fool,' is believed to be derived from the word 'logger' which was used colloquially to refer to a block of wood for hobbling horses. Loggerheads itself takes its name from the Loggerheads pub, formerly known as the Three Loggerheads, whose sign featured two fools' heads and a third, that of an onlooker.

Wars of the Roses

But it was at Boreheath, just to the west of the village, where history was made, for it was there that the first major battle of the Wars of the Roses was fought. This involved an ongoing dispute between the House of Lancaster, led by King Henry VI, and the House of York, led by Richard, Duke of York. As an experienced soldier and leader, Richard believed he had a better claim to the throne than Henry and duly expected to inherit the crown; when the King sired a son and heir, however, Richard realised that he would have to resort to force.

Queen Margaret

The year is 1459: Richard's allies are fragmented all over England, and to consolidate his forces he orders Neville, Earl of Salisbury, to march from his castle in Yorkshire to his own pile in Ludlow, about 40 miles (64km) south of Boreheath. Aware of this march, Queen Margaret directs James Touchet, Lord Audley, to intercept Salisbury's army.

Knowing that the road to Ludlow will take Salisbury through a defile near Boreheath, Audley assembles 10,000 soldiers on the heath overlooking the road. On Sunday, 23 September, the two sides oppose each other across the valley, Salisbury on the slopes where Audley's Cross now stands and Audley on the other side. Salisbury has nothing in the way of firearms, and is heavily outnumbered. And so, the scene is set for a rout.

Battle Tactics

But Salisbury has other ideas. He senses that Audley is over-confident and that he may be tempted into a glorious cavalry charge, to impress Queen

LOGGERHEADS

Margaret and to destroy his enemy. To make it even more tempting, Salisbury feigns a retreat by withdrawing his pikemen from the front, leaving an opening for a charge. Seizing this opportunity, Audley orders his cavalry down the hill but underestimates the difficulty of ascending the steep, muddy slope of the brook at the bottom. Exposed and vulnerable, the horses are no match for Salisbury's archers who have been waiting in the wings. The result is unequivocal. Twice Audley's forces charge and twice they are mown down. A third assault involves more than 4,000 infantry. Audley is slain in the bitter hand-to-hand fighting which ensues, and today his cross still marks the spot where he died.

The battle lasted all day. By nightfall, more than 2,000 Lancastrians lay dead or dying on the blood-soaked battlefield, while Yorkist casualties numbered just 56. But ultimately it was to no avail; after 30 years of war the Lancastrians kept the throne.

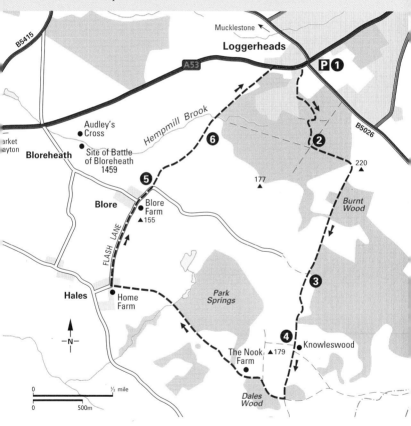

WALK 26 DIRECTIONS

❶ Head along the A53 in the direction of Market Drayton and take the first left along Kestrel Drive. Just after The Robins head left along the gravel track down the back of some houses. When you reach the end of a cul-de-sac, go left on a wide woodland track. After skirting a large, deep hollow turn right. At a clearing bear left past an iron bar across a wide track and, at the fork, go right, past the football pitch, then turn left uphill to reach a major path junction.

2 Take the fourth path on your left and where this finally runs out, follow a narrow path through the undergrowth to reach a wide gravel track. Turn right through the gate and continue for 0.5 mile (800m), until the main track goes right.

WHAT TO LOOK OUT FOR

Although it's difficult to actually walk across the battlefield today, the surrounding landscape still includes many of the same features that were present in 1459, such as lanes, villages, hedges and woodlands. Most obvious of these is Hempmill Brook, across which Audley's army charged. The site is considered especially important because it's one of only a handful of medieval battlefields to have escaped modern development.

3 Head over a stile and along the footpath with a hedge to your right-hand side. At the bottom of the field bear right towards the right-hand corner of the bank of trees. Go through a gate here and head up towards Knowleswood farm (which is now derelict) and another gate.

4 Continue straight ahead and, at the bottom of the field, go right over a stile and drop down through a small dip. At the bottom of the dip go through a gate and head right along a concrete track. At a fork go left to The Nook Farm and, after a mile (1.6km) reach Home Farm. Turn right here along Flash Lane and up the gentle hill to Blore Farm. When you get to a junction

WHERE TO EAT AND DRINK

The Peel Arms at the village of Ashley, just over a mile away from Loggerheads, serves a variety of home-cooked dishes Wednesday–Sunday evenings and weekend lunchtimes. There's also a very pleasant beer garden in the summer.

keep going straight and, after 200yds (183m), head left through a hedge over a stile. Follow this hedge right to a stile in the right-hand corner of the field. This stile probably provides the best vantage point from which to view the main battlefield, now private farm land, which was centred on the shallow valley to your left.

5 Continue to the bottom right-hand corner of the next field before bearing diagonally right across another field to the right-hand end of a bank of trees. Cross the small stile and follow the faint track straight across the middle of the next field to another stile.

6 Follow the path through a young plantation to a fence ahead and cross a stile. Keep following the faint track alongside a wood to your right and, when you come to a clearing, head diagonally across the field to the left-hand end of the trees. At the corner of this field, cross a stile and footbridge to a wide track, which you follow right and up the hill to a large, lone oak at the top. Turn left here to cross a stile back on to the A53.

WHILE YOU'RE THERE

It's said that Queen Margaret watched the defeat of the Lancastrian forces from the church tower at Mucklestone. Fearing for her safety, she made plans for her escape, instructing the local blacksmith, William Skelhorn, to put the shoes on her horse the wrong way round, to disguise her escape. Unfortunately for Skelhorn, the Queen had him executed so that he couldn't reveal the deception. The anvil supposedly used by Skelhorn was preserved and still stands in front of St Mary's in Mucklestone today.

A Loop Around the Hanchurch Hills

*A walk from Swynnerton Old Park, discovering
the legacy of Hanchurch's watery heritage.*

DISTANCE 7 miles (11.3km)	**MINIMUM TIME** 2hrs 30min
ASCENT/GRADIENT 420ft (128m) ▲▲▲	**LEVEL OF DIFFICULTY** ✦✦✦
PATHS Gravel tracks, field paths and roads, 1 stile	
LANDSCAPE Woodland, farmland and village	
SUGGESTED MAP OS Explorer 243 Market Drayton	
START/FINISH Grid reference: SJ 839399	
DOG FRIENDLINESS Must be kept on lead near livestock	
PARKING Hanchurch Hills Picnic Place car park	
PUBLIC TOILETS None en route	

The walk begins in Swynnerton Old Park, near the first of this walk's water towers. Of course, it's not just coincidence that there are so many water towers in the area; the sandstone strata of Meecebrook Valley, formed during the Triassic period, is capable of providing 1.5 million gallons (7 million litres) of clean water a day.

Satisfying the Demand for Water

At the end of the 19th century, in response to an increase in demand for high quality water, thanks in part to the new fashion for indoor baths, the Staffordshire Potteries Water Board built the Hatton Water Works, a project which took the best part of 20 years to complete. Water was pumped directly to Hanchurch Reservoir (now Hanchurch Pools), which then supplied water to Newcastle, Stoke and the Trent Valley.

Restored Tower

Today, water is still pumped at Hatton, but electricity has now replaced steam and the Grade II listed, yellow- and red-brick buildings have been converted into various luxury apartments. The carefully restored water tower just north of Swynnerton, however, gives an idea of quite how impressive these Italianate-style buildings must once have been, with their red-brick columns, circular windows and triumphal archways superimposed on warm, yellow-brick façades. The Swynnerton tower itself has been ingeniously rebuilt as a house, with its vast windows and spiral staircase in the middle, up to the first floor.

Historic Buildings

Swynnerton, meanwhile, has more than its fair share of historic buildings for a village so small. The oldest of these is 13th-century St Mary's Church. Apart from the statue of Christ (see What To Look Out For), the feature of most interest is undoubtedly the simple Norman doorway, which nonetheless has a detailed beakhead moulding. Over the road is a Roman Catholic church dedicated to Our Lady of the Assumption and built from local stone by Gilbert Blount, who tried to imbue his designs with a distinctly Gothic feel.

The chapel itself is attached to Swynnerton Hall which, though not obvious from the village, dominates the Swynnerton skyline from the south. The hall was built in 1725 to replace an earlier manor house demolished by Cromwell in the Civil War. Its owner, Sir John Fitzherbert, supported the Royalist cause. His grandson Basil built the hall seen today.

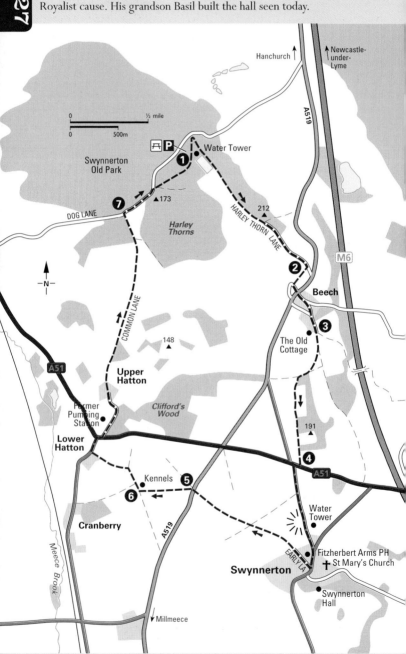

WALK 27 DIRECTIONS

1 From the car park take the left fork along a gravel track, which is Harley Thorn Lane. Then turn left again at the next fork past a derelict water tower and reservoir on your right. After 650yds (594m) go through a gate and continue ahead along the metalled road.

2 Just before the A519 go right up a gravel track and, shortly after, at a hairpin in another road, head left, going downhill. At the next fork, go right. At the road junction turn left and follow the road until you come to a fork just after The Old Cottage on your right.

3 Go right here, following a sign for the Hanchurch Walk, and keep following the main path, ignoring the public footpath signs to the left. At the obvious gravel bridleway head right up into the woods and, at the top of the woods, carry straight on, following the track to the A51.

4 Turn right, then take the first left, following the minor road towards Swynnerton. Just past the Fitzherbert Arms on the right, turn right along Early Lane. At the end of the road, keep going straight

along a signed footpath. At a major path junction, go straight on, in the same direction, across the middle of a wide field. Continue on this public footpath through three more fields to the A519.

5 Cross the road with care and then carry on by going left in the next field, beside the hedge. Continue to the end of the field, go through some trees and then right to the stile and a gravel drive.

6 Turn right past the kennels and, at Lower Hatton Stables, turn right along the road to the A51. Take care crossing this road, heading right then taking the first left, past Lower Hatton Pumping Station, now private residences. Follow this road to Upper Hatton and then carry on straight along Common Lane all the way back to Swynnerton Old Park.

7 At Dog Lane turn right and, after 400yds (366m), as the road eases round to the left up a slight hill, turn right up the dirt track. Head left at the fork immediately after the start of the track. When you reach a clearing with a car park and picnic site, make for the left of the water tower, continuing along the track back to the start.

Overleaf: Trig point, Swynnerton (Walk 27)

A Wander Around Wedgwood Country

A gentle, short walk exploring the life and times
of the Staffordshire Potteries' most famous son.

28

DISTANCE 3.25 miles (5.3km)   **MINIMUM TIME** 1hr 15min

ASCENT/GRADIENT 180ft (55m) ▲▲▲   **LEVEL OF DIFFICULTY** +♦♦

PATHS Roads, gravel tracks and tow paths, 3 stiles

LANDSCAPE Village, farmland and canal

SUGGESTED MAP OS Explorer 258 Stoke-on-Trent

START/FINISH Grid reference: SJ 889395

DOG FRIENDLINESS Must be kept on lead near livestock

PARKING Roadside parking near Wedgwood visitor centre entrance

PUBLIC TOILETS Wedgwood visitor centre (customers only)

During the 18th and 19th centuries, white stoneware was all the rage in polite society, thanks in part to an influx of expensive white china from the Orient. In the quest for a cheaper alternative, potters spent decades experimenting with powdered flint from the local mills (see Walk 12). Flint, when mixed with clay, helps to whiten it, but there were so many problems with the process and such a high level of wastage that for a time English china was more expensive than silver. In the 1760s, however, Josiah Wedgwood perfected cream ware and a few years later, when Queen Charlotte purchased an entire tea set, marketing genius Josiah cannily changed the name to Queen's Ware. The rest, as they say, is pottery.

Josiah Wedgwood

The Wedgwood family came from Burslem, a district of what is now Stoke-on-Trent. Craftsman Gilbert Wedgwood was recorded as the first Master Potter in the family in 1640 – and his most famous descendant, Josiah, was born in 1730. Josiah worked in his father's pottery from the age of nine, and in 1744 he was apprenticed to his older brother Thomas. An attack of smallpox seriously reduced Josiah's output (his right leg later had to be amputated as a result of the illness) but the time it gave him to research and experiment in his chosen craft stood him in good stead in later years.

Broke the Mould

After a number of partnerships Josiah set up his own pottery in Burslem in 1759. Until then pottery had been something of a cottage industry, but Wedgwood broke the mould, building – for the first time ever – a pottery factory. And rather than rely on family members, his idea was to pay people to work in the factory, with materials and tools he supplied. This made the whole production process so much more efficient and, ultimately, more lucrative.

A decade later, with business booming, Josiah Wedgwood built a bigger factory in Burslem which he called Etruria (at the time, Greek vases were believed to be Etruscan in origin). This became a model for other pottery manufacturers. Here he applied rigorous, scientific techniques to producing new, innovative pottery. The results of his efforts can still be purchased today and include Jasperware (characterised by unglazed, pale blue stoneware with white relief portraits or classical scenes) and black basalt ware, also known as Egyptian ware, a hard stone-like material used for vases and busts of historical figures.

But of course, when Josiah Wedgwood died in Etruria in 1795 his legacy wasn't just limited to porcelain. His success, vision and innovative business practices made him a leading figure of the Industrial Revolution and his impact on the local countryside was immense, not least because of the hundreds of miles of canals that he was – at least in part – responsible for, including the Trent and Mersey and Caldon canals.

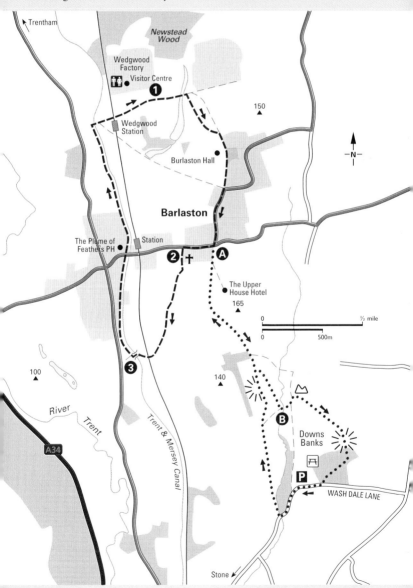

WALK 28 DIRECTIONS

1 From the visitor centre drive, head left across the lake and then right up the drive towards Barlaston Hall. Go past this hall and continue along the metalled road as far as the crossroads in Barlaston. At the crossroads turn right and after 250yds (229m), just past the Church of St John the Baptist on your left, head left along a wide gravel track.

2 The track passes through a broad expanse of open farmland, with sweeping (if not altogether dramatic) views of the Trent and Mersey canal to the right and, beyond, the flood plain of the Trent Valley. After about 800yds (732m), at the third gate, go right on a less obvious path around the edge of the field to reach a stile. After crossing the stile head right along a wide track, then cross the railway via an underpass, before

bearing right to a bridge over the canal. Go over the bridge and take the steps down to the left.

3 At the bottom of the steps head left and then follow the canal all the way to the first bridge (at Barlaston) and then the second (at Wedgwood Station). Head left here, up to the metalled road, and then right, back towards the visitor centre.

Downs Banks

This short loop includes impressive views from Downs Banks.
See map and information panel for Walk 28

29

DISTANCE 3.5 miles (5.7km)   **MINIMUM TIME** 1hr 30min
ASCENT/GRADIENT 656ft (200m) ▲▲▲   **LEVEL OF DIFFICULTY** ✦✦✦

WALK 29 DIRECTIONS
(Walk 28 options)

Leave the main route at the crossroads, Point **Ⓐ**, and go straight across, following signs to The Upper House Hotel. After 100yds (91m) stay straight along a track, ignoring the metalled road up to the hotel to your left. Continue along the bottom of the field as far as the swing gate and then head diagonally left across the next field following an obvious dirt path.

At the far side of this field cross a stile and carry on above the next field, until you get to another stile and the edge of Downs Banks. After crossing this stile, make your way along the top of the wide ridge for 100yds (91m) and fork left at a bridleway marker down a track to a stream. A little further on, cross the stream on the stepping stones to reach a path junction. Go second left (not hard left) through a gate, Point **Ⓑ**. Head left and then, after 100yds (91m), go hard right up the steep spur of the hill.

Follow this trail all the way to the viewfinder at the top, and then continue along the top of the eastern bank until beyond a gate it forks right and drops steadily back down to a gate and Wash Dale Lane. At the road turn right, following it round to the left to a small footbridge by a ford. Head immediately right, back into Downs Banks and, after 150yds (137m), go left up a stepped track to the top, leaving the stream behind.

Walk along the top until you leave the woods behind. When you get to a fence ahead of you, go left over the stile and retrace your steps to rejoin the main route, Point **Ⓐ**.

WHAT TO LOOK OUT FOR
Downs Banks were once crossed by an ancient packhorse trail from the East Midlands to Chester. They remained common land until the end of the 18th century, when they were enclosed by hedges for farming, traces of which can still be seen, particularly near the picnic sites. The land was used to grow hops bound for the nearby Joules brewery. In 1950, when the area was threatened with industrialisation from Meaford Power Station, 160 acres (65ha) were purchased by John Joules & Sons, endowed by public subscription and given to the National Trust. Today, a memorial stone of Cornish granite stands near the south corner of the park to commemorate this presentation, and to serve as a tribute to those who lost their lives during World War II.

Tutbury's Crystal Ball

*A short stroll tracing fortunes found
and lost in this industrious little village.*

DISTANCE 2.75 miles (4.4km)   MINIMUM TIME 1hr

ASCENT/GRADIENT 88ft (27m) ▲▲▲   LEVEL OF DIFFICULTY +++

PATHS Road and field track, 11 stiles

LANDSCAPE Town, farmland and riverside

SUGGESTED MAP OS Explorer 245 The National Forest

START/FINISH Grid reference: SK 213294

DOG FRIENDLINESS Keep on lead at all times

PARKING Tutbury Mill picnic site

PUBLIC TOILETS At town car park in Tutbury

WALK 30 DIRECTIONS

The village of Tutbury, just across the border from neighbouring Derbyshire, boasts a long history of making, and finding, money, and nowhere is this more obvious than at the picnic site near the start of the walk. In 1781, a five-storey mill was built here on the Mill Fleam, an artificial braid of the River Dove. Originally it was a cotton mill employing more than 300 workers, with two 14ft (4.3m) waterwheels powering an astonishing 7,000 spindles. Mill Farm, across the road, was originally a warehouse.

After more than 100 years the cotton mill closed but, in 1890,

Henry Newton acquired it for making plaster of Paris from gypsum, mined in the Fauld Hills 2 miles (3.2km) west of Tutbury. In its purest form, gypsum is known as alabaster and because it is relatively soft, it is ideal for ornamental carving. Gypsum is also used for brewing pale ale, which accounts for the flourishing beer industry in Burton on Trent, 5 miles (8km) to the south. Production of plaster continued until 1968, when the mill was demolished, but British Gypsum still mines in the Fauld Hills, extracting some 650,000 tons of gypsum annually.

Despite all this hard work and industry over the centuries, there were easier ways to find your fortune in Tutbury. In 1831, men excavating the river to improve the flow of water to the mill found several hundred medieval coins. The river was quarantined to prevent looting and a major dig was conducted. Remarkably, more than 100,000 silver coins were recovered, some of which can still be seen at the Stoke city museum

WHERE TO EAT AND DRINK
The Bay Tree Delicatessen serves a variety of sandwiches, snacks, home-made cakes and drinks. For something a bit more substantial, Ye Olde Dog & Partridge boasts two good restaurants. It is also one of England's oldest coaching inns, dating from the 15th century.

in Hanley. The question was, where had the cash come from?

The answer lay in a battle fought and lost over 500 years before by Thomas, Duke of Lancaster and Lord of Tutbury Castle. Thomas sided with the Scots against his cousin Edward II in the early 1300s, so the King attacked the castle to teach him a lesson. Thomas lay in wait at Burton Bridge, but was outflanked and duly defeated by Edward in 1322. His fortune was smuggled out of the castle, but the horses floundered crossing the river. When it was found again in 1831, it was claimed by the Crown.

WHAT TO LOOK OUT FOR

The elaborate west door of St Mary's Church in Tutbury, built c1160, is a fine example of Norman craftsmanship and is believed to have been made from local alabaster.

These days Tutbury is known more for its fine Georgian crystal than its bloody medieval heritage. The first glassworks were founded at the height of the Industrial Revolution, and today there are two in the village, both with excellent factory shops. At Georgian Crystal, glass is crafted right there in the shop.

From the picnic site, head right at the roundabout into the town. Stay right at the first fork and, after 150yds (137m), head right up a footpath to St Mary's Church. Pass the church and the castle entrance to the main road. Go right here and, at the top of a short hill, follow the footpath signs to the right.

Go down this footpath to the flood plain. Walk through a swing gate, then head diagonally right

to the far right-hand corner of the field. At this corner head right into the next field and then left over a stile into another field. Continue diagonally right to another obvious stile-footbridge-stile. Cut off the left corner of the field, aiming for the middle of the left-hand hedge. Cross the stile here and walk straight across the long meadow, heading for the left of some distant farmhouses. After 600yds (549m), at the meeting of two hedges, cross a double stile and continue with a hedge to your left. Cross another double stile at the end of this field and keep following the hedge to your left.

As you reach Boundary House, to your left, go right along the obvious concrete track back towards Fauld Cottage Farm. Head to the right of the farm gate, off the concrete, to a stile. Over the stile, head straight across the middle of the field to an obvious gate on the far side. After the gate, head straight towards the castle, back the way you came. At the far left corner of the meadow, very close to the river, cross the stile and skirt left around the bank beneath a line of trees. Cross Mill Fleam to the weir.

Head sharp right into an open meadow. Follow the faint path along Mill Fleam back to the picnic site and the car park on the far side.

WHILE YOU'RE THERE

The vast earthworks of Tutbury Castle date from c1070, but much of the stonework that exists today dates from the 15th century. Mary, Queen of Scots, was imprisoned here by Elizabeth I, and during the Civil War it was a Royalist stronghold, after which it was demolished by Cromwell's troops.

30

The Secret of the Hanbury Crater

Investigating the haunting site of the biggest, non-nuclear explosion of the Second World War.

31

DISTANCE 4.75 miles (7.7km)	**MINIMUM TIME** 2hrs
ASCENT/GRADIENT 240ft (73m) ▲▲▲	**LEVEL OF DIFFICULTY** ✦✦✦

PATHS Meadow tracks and bridleways, 34 stiles

LANDSCAPE Farmland and bomb crater

SUGGESTED MAP OS Explorer 245 The National Forest

START/FINISH Grid reference: SK 171279

DOG FRIENDLINESS Must be kept on lead near livestock

PARKING St Werburgh's Church car park

PUBLIC TOILETS None en route

The history of Hanbury starts with the legend of St Werburgh. During the 7th century AD Werburgh, daughter of pagan King Wulfere of Mercia, founded nunneries at Repton, Trentham, Weedon and Hanbury, the latter believed to have been situated to the east of what is now St Werburgh's Church.

St Werburgh

Legend has it that when Werburgh died she was buried at Trentham, but her body was stolen back by the people of Hanbury and buried in a new shrine near the nunnery. As a direct result Hanbury became a major centre for Christianity for well over a century. When the Danes invaded in AD 875, Werburgh's body was again moved, this time to Chester for safe keeping, and it was there, in the cathedral, that she was finally laid to rest.

A Wartime Tragedy

Today, however, Hanbury is known for a much more recent tragedy. At 11am on 27 November, 1944, the village witnessed the largest explosion caused by a conventional weapon in either world war; only the atomic bombs at Hiroshima and Nagasaki were bigger. In all, 70 people were killed in the blast, and 18 bodies were never recovered.

A Distant Rumble

The reason for the explosion is unclear, although the site is hard to miss, marked as it is by a crater more than 0.25 mile (400m) across and 100yds (91m) deep. The area around Hanbury is rich in gypsum and alabaster and a number of exhausted mine shafts became convenient storage depots for high explosives during the war. RAF personnel and Italian prisoners of war dispatched this arsenal with heightening urgency as the Allied offensive in Europe got underway, and it's thought that carelessness, inexperience and cost-cutting all had a part to play on that fateful November morning.

The first the villagers knew about it was a distant rumble before the explosion proper, which blackened the sky as tens of thousands of tons of soil and rocks were blasted into the surrounding landscape. An entire farm, including its occupants and livestock, disappeared completely, and dozens of underground munitions workers – both British and Italian – were killed. A reservoir for the nearby plaster works burst its dam, unleashing 6 million gallons (27 million litres) of water, boulders, mud and trees on to the factory below, killing 27 workers. The explosion could be heard from London and was recorded as an earth tremor as far away as Geneva.

Today, nature has healed the scars on the landscape as hawthorn, larch, and silver birch have re-colonised both the crater and the surrounding area, providing a habitat for – among other things – a vast colony of rabbits. There's still a gypsum works to the north, below which is an extensive system of mines spread over 10 square miles (26sq km).

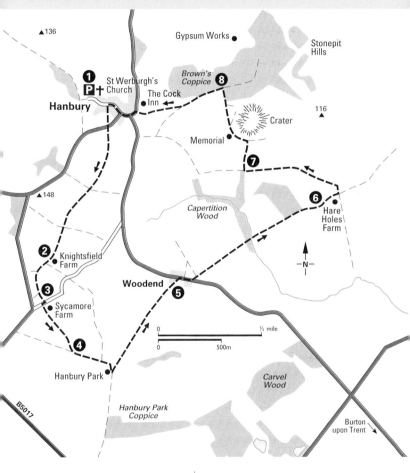

WALK 31 DIRECTIONS

1 From the car park, go back along Church Lane and after 150yds (137m), go right through a car park and through a gate. Cross the field to a pair of stiles over a road and continue across the field to a gate, then to the corner of a hedge. Keeping this hedge to your right, head for Knightsfield Farm.

2 Go through the farm courtyard and along a rough surfaced track.

As it bears to the right, follow a footpath sign, left, across stiles, keeping the hedge to your left. At a turning circle on a driveway go straight across to a footbridge before continuing, with the hedge to your left to reach the road.

3 Turn right, then after 80 yards (73m) go left at the footpath sign beside the building. Cross the yard into the field ahead to the stile at the bottom. Continue up the next field, crossing the stile at the top.

4 Where the hedge goes left, follow it across another stile and, via fields, aim for the imposing brick buildings of Hanbury Park. Go through a series of metal swing gates into the farm courtyard, then head left at the bridleway signpost and through a wide gate away from the farm. Continue on the bridleway to Woodend.

WHERE TO EAT AND DRINK

The Cock Inn is a charming little pub with picnic tables and good views. It also has newspaper reports of the tragedy lining the walls for those who are interested in finding out more. It serves a wide variety of bar snacks and meals, and is open all day at weekends and from 5pm Monday to Friday.

---

5 At the road head right for 100yds (91m) then go left over a stile, making for a stile in the fence ahead/right. Head diagonally left across a field to a stile, then continue straight across the next field to a stile. Cross Capertition Wood to an open field, continuing with a hedge to the left, up a hill, across stiles, then down to another. At the end of the field cross one more.

6 Skirting to the left of the farm, climb over a succession of

stiles before turning sharp left immediately after an iron gate. Once across the stile in the corner, go ahead through three more fields, following waymarkers past a small pond. Drop down to the right-hand end of a bank of trees.

WHILE YOU'RE THERE

Apart from the core of the west tower and the 13th-century arcades with round piers, St Werburgh's Church is of little interest architecturally, having been almost entirely rebuilt in the late 19th century. But if the church is open (and it usually is), look for the window in the south aisle featuring a memorial to those who died in the explosion, made using fragments of 14th-century stained glass.

---

7 At a path junction turn right up a short hill via kissing gates, towards trees. Head round to the left to see the crater, now re-colonised by nature. Follow the path round to the left, past the memorial stone, to a bridleway leading away from it.

8 At the end of this bridleway, head left across a field, keeping the hedge to your right. Go through a kissing gate in the hedge ahead and continue straight ahead to a gate at the top. When you reach the end of the hedge on your left go through a gate and a stile to return to Hanbury.

WHAT TO LOOK OUT FOR

The memorial just to the south of the crater is made of fine white granite, a gift from the Commandant of the Italian Air Force Supply Depot at Novara in north-west Italy. The stone lists the names of the people killed, including those whose bodies were never recovered. It is a poignant reminder of the tragedy.

Discovering Stafford Castle

*A short walk from Stafford town around
one of the county's oldest monuments.*

DISTANCE *4 miles (6.4km)*   **MINIMUM TIME** *1hr 30min*

ASCENT/GRADIENT *240ft (73m)* ▲▲▲   **LEVEL OF DIFFICULTY** ✦✦✦

PATHS *Pavement, gravel tracks and grass trails*

LANDSCAPE *Town, golf course, hilltop and farmland*

SUGGESTED MAP *OS Explorer 244 Cannock Chase*

START/FINISH *Grid reference: SJ 918233*

DOG FRIENDLINESS *Keep on lead near livestock*

PARKING *Pay car parks in town centre*

PUBLIC TOILETS *Stafford Castle visitor centre and in town centre*

In the 11th century, a castle was built on the hill to the west of Stafford by William the Conqueror to keep rebellious Saxons in check. It was at this time that the substantial earthworks around the present-day castle were built. They involved a series of avenues, deep ditches, steep slopes and an impressive motte, or steep-sided earth mound, at the centre of the castle complex. Today, it's possible to take a tour of these earthworks by following a series of excellent information panels around the site, and with the help of sketches it's not hard to imagine how the castle might have looked.

Hilltop Home and Military Headquarters

Initially, the site would have resembled more of a hilltop settlement, with wooden ramparts built in concentric rings behind a series of deep ditches. The castle proper would have been a three-storey timber keep on the motte and would have doubled as the lord's residence and his military headquarters. The timber may have been plastered and painted to look like stone, to fool any approaching enemies.

Stone Castle

It wasn't until the middle of the 14th century that Ralph, Lord Stafford, built the first stone castle on the site. It stayed in the family until 1521, when Henry VIII had Edward Stafford executed on a dubious charge of treason (he actually had a distant claim to the throne). The Staffords recovered their property and titles 25 years later but failed to recover their fortune. By the end of the 16th century, the castle was in ruins and remained so until the Civil War broke out in 1642. Isabel, Lady Stafford, was requested by Charles I to defend the castle against Parliamentary forces, and successfully resisted months of siege.

The castle continued to be neglected until Sir George Jerningham had the ruin cleared of debris in the early 19th century and rebuilt the eastern towers in what was an early example of Gothic revival architecture. The lords and ladies of the mid-19th century were a romantic bunch and liked nothing better than to dress up their summer piles as Gothic follies complete with pointed arches and mock battlements.

Visitor Centre

Alas, Sir George never got around to the rest of the renovation and the castle has been more or less neglected ever since. In 1961, a boy playing on the remaining stonework was tragically killed by a collapsing window. The reaction of the local council was to demolish the upper part of the building, although they resisted calls to demolish the entire thing on the basis that it may still contain some of the original 14th-century masonry. Indeed, excavations begun in 1974 have shown this to be the case. Today, the castle is preserved, with a visitor centre providing a useful insight into the chronicle of the castle, and in particular its Norman founders.

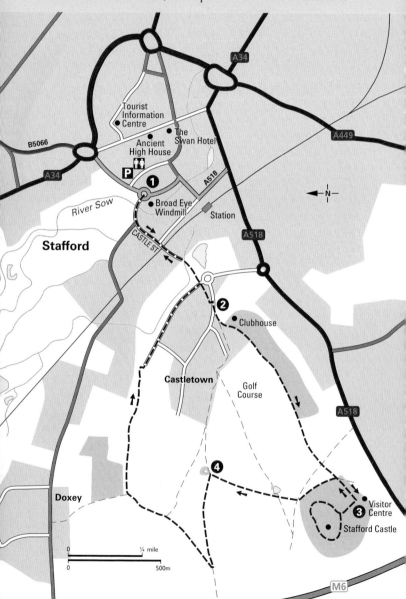

WALK 32 DIRECTIONS

① From the roundabout by Broad Eye Windmill head away from the town, over the river. After 100yds (91m) go left along Castle Street and over the railway bridge to the roundabout. Cross and walk along the path to the next road.

WHERE TO EAT AND DRINK

There are numerous tea shops, bakeries, restaurants and bars to choose from in the town centre, from the exotic to traditional pub food, but you can't go wrong with The Swan Hotel, a former coaching inn dating from 1750 which still features the original carriage entrance. The brasserie serves an extensive and varied menu, 12–10pm daily.

---

② Cross over, turn right, then bear left by a line of trees, going left again at a footpath sign and keeping the houses to your right. Follow the gravel track all the way up through the middle of the golf course and, at the very top, keep going straight across the field ahead of you, following a faint grass trail to a gap in the woods. Turn left for a path along the edge of the trees to the castle visitor centre. The centre makes an ideal starting point for any visit, packed as it is with information on the Norman Conquest and featuring a short film on the history of the castle itself. There's also a shop selling snacks, souvenirs and guides, not just on the castle, but on other castles, churches and historical buildings throughout Staffordshire.

③ After following the castle's self-guided walk (0.75 mile / 1.2km) go back the way you came, along the bottom of the wood to the gap, and skirt left around the outside of the wood. At the corner of the wood, go through the hedge and head

right. Continue down the field edge path with the hedge on your right. Descending through these fields also serves to illustrate how tough it must have been for Saxon forces to charge in the opposite direction; even assuming they survived the onslaught of arrows from Norman long-bows, by the time they got anywhere near the castle they'd have been absolutely spent.

WHILE YOU'RE THERE

Built in 1595 during the reign of Elizabeth I, Stafford's Ancient High House is today the largest timber-framed townhouse in England. Charles I stayed here in 1642 at the beginning of the Civil War and the following year, when the town was captured and the castle besieged by the Parliamentarians, it became a prison for Royalist officers. It's open to visitors Tue–Sat, 10am–4pm, throughout the year.

---

④ When you come to a junction and a hedge ahead, go left and two fields on turn hard right on a wide track downhill. Follow this round to the right and back towards Stafford. When the track runs out, bear right on to the road and then left across a roundabout. Just before the next roundabout (Point **②**) head left, retracing your steps back into Stafford.

WHAT TO LOOK OUT FOR

Although the castle is barely 75yds (69m) higher than the surrounding countryside, it commands surprisingly good views in every direction. From the top, looking out over the earthworks, it's easy to see how enemy forces could be spotted approaching from miles away, and how easy it must have been to defend.

Through the Shugborough Estate

An easy walk gives you a chance to appreciate the architectural history of Staffordshire's greatest country house.

33

DISTANCE 4.25 miles (6.8km)   **MINIMUM TIME** 1hr 45min

ASCENT/GRADIENT 180ft (55m) ▲▲▲   **LEVEL OF DIFFICULTY** ✦✦✦

PATHS Gravel tracks, roads and tow paths

LANDSCAPE Forest, country park and canal

SUGGESTED MAP OS Explorer 244 Cannock Chase

START/FINISH Grid reference: SK 004205

DOG FRIENDLINESS Must be kept on lead near main roads and in park

PARKING Seven Springs car park

PUBLIC TOILETS None en route

Shugborough, a 900-acre (365ha) estate on the edge of Cannock Chase, is without doubt the grandest stately home in Staffordshire. As the ancestral pile of the Earls of Lichfield for more than 300 years, it was home to Thomas Patrick Anson, Fifth Earl of Lichfield until his death in 2005. He was better known as the world famous photographer Patrick Lichfield, who also happens to be second cousin to the Queen.

Grand Stately Home

Originally built in 1693 as a small country manor, it has been altered and added to by successive generations of the Anson family, and by two people in particular: Thomas Anson (1695–1773) and his brother George (1697–1762). Thomas, well-travelled and well-educated, inherited the house in 1720, and made major changes over the next 50 years, while the most significant alteration, or at least the one most apparent from the outside, was the addition of a magnificent, eight-columned ionic portico designed by Samuel Wyatt in 1794. Much of this work was paid for out of George's own fortune: during his lifetime he had earned considerable fame and riches as a naval officer by capturing a Spanish treasure galleon. He later went on to become an Admiral.

As a well-travelled man, Thomas would have been very aware of what was considered good taste throughout his dealings with architects, and the house as we see it today is testimony to his ideals and what was considered the height of fashion for much of the 18th century. This, it's important to remember, was the age of reason, when industry and science were starting to take over the world; architects and their employers were keen to reflect this idea in their country piles, and the geometric simplicity of ancient Greek and Roman architecture seemed like a logical choice. It embodied the ideals of man being at the centre of the universe, taming nature with his new-found knowledge.

The gardens, too, were ordered and regimented, set out in a formal geometric pattern with the house at the centre of the estate, and, by implication, the universe. It was the same ideal that made classical motifs on Wedgwood pottery so enduring, and it's no surprise that Thomas Anson was a patron of the famous potter. Almost as a direct consequence of this insistence on law and order in gardens and architecture, the architects of the 19th century instigated a backlash against reason: romance was king, disorder was beauty, and the so-called 'Gothic' style enjoyed a revival in mansions and follies across England.

Held in Trust

Today, from the outside, the mansion is much the same as it must have been during Thomas Anson's day. In 1966, following the death of the Fourth Earl of Lichfield, the estate was given to the National Trust; since then it has been managed jointly by the Trust and Staffordshire County Council; the house isn't open all year but as the route of the walk is on either a public bridleway or established rights of way it can be completed at any time of year.

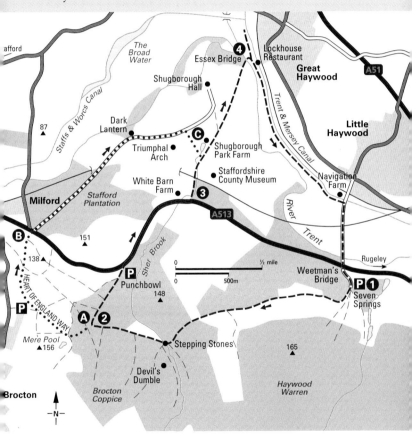

WALK 33 DIRECTIONS

❶ Take the right-hand path at the end of Seven Springs car park and continue right at a junction shortly after. Follow a wide gravel track, ignoring all paths to the left or right, and continue as far as Stepping Stones. Cross the stream here and head right as far as the major T-junction.

33

❷ Head right here, following the Staffordshire Way bridleway sign. Continue along a wide gravel track, again ignoring less obvious paths to the left or right, as far as the A513. Cross the road carefully and follow it right for 400yds (366m) before turning left at a road entrance to Shugborough Hall.

❸ Follow the metalled road past the Staffordshire County Museum and the main car park and ticket office to the Hall. Here you will also find the Craft Workshops and the Walled Garden. The garden was established in 1805 as a horticultural centre of excellence and completely restored in 2007 to its original state (they are even growing historic varieties of fruit and vegetables that are now quite rare today). A little beyond Shugborough Park Farm, ignore a more direct path left to the house itself and instead follow the bridleway all the way to Essex Bridge. It's worth pausing to take a closer look at the façade. From close range it's interesting to note that the columns aren't made of stone at all, but are instead made of wood which has been clad with slate and painted to look like stone,

a solution that would have been considerably cheaper.

❹ By way of a short diversion, just 350yds (320m) to the north of Essex Bridge, heading left along the tow path, is the junction of the Trent and Mersey and the Staffordshire and Worcestershire canals. The toll-keeper's cottage has disappeared, but a toll-house with arched windows and a kiosk still remain on the south side of the latter. Go across the bridge and head right along the canal (cross Essex Bridge and the canal to reach the Lockhouse Restaurant on the left). Follow the tow path for a mile (1.6km) and, at Navigation Farm, head right on the metalled road. Carry on over Weetman's Bridge, cross the A513 carefully, and continue up a short drive back to the car park.

WHAT TO LOOK OUT FOR

There are no fewer than eight monuments of national importance to be seen in the 900 acres (365ha) of parkland around Shugborough, but the most obvious of these en route are the Dark Lantern and the Triumphal Arch. These follies were designed by, among others, James 'Athenian' Stuart, a classicist whose popularity reflected the tastes of the time. Originally built by the Earl of Essex to gain access to Cannock Chase for hunting, the Essex Bridge is the longest packhorse bridge in England, and has never been widened.

WHILE YOU'RE THERE

In addition to the house itself, the estate features a working farm museum in a second building designed by Samuel Wyatt, with demonstrations of farmhouse cooking, milking, and bread, butter and cheese-making by guides in period dress. The old servants' quarters, meanwhile, house the County Museum where costumed actors re-create what life was like on the estate a hundred years ago.

An Extension to Shugborough

An alternative route through the impressive grounds of Shugborough.
See map and information panel for Walk 33

34

DISTANCE *5 miles (8km)* **MINIMUM TIME** *2hrs 15min*

ASCENT/GRADIENT *175ft (53m)* ▲▲▲ **LEVEL OF DIFFICULTY** +++

WALK 34 DIRECTIONS
(Walk 33 option)

At the track junction, Point **A**, leave Walk 33 and head left following the footpath sign to Mere Pool. When you reach the junction of a number of paths keep going in the same direction, now following a section of the Heart of England Way down a slight, and remarkably straight, incline.

At the next path junction, near the bottom of this path, continue straight on, down the hill, shortly passing a house to your left. Go past the wooden barrier and through a long, narrow car park. At the far end veer right for a wide and well-used track.

Follow this up a slight hill on to a plateau and continue to another fork by a small pond. Go right here, again following the less obvious of the two tracks. Soon after you start to drop down the other side of the small plateau, you reach another fork of two dirt trails. Head right on the narrower and less-walked route and continue down through the woods to the main entrance of Shugborough Hall on the edge of Milford Common, Point **B**.

Take care when crossing the A513 and continue through the gates along a main driveway.

Follow this for 1.25 miles (2km) through woodland and then out into open parkland past the Dark Lantern statue (also known as the Lanthorn of Demosthenes). At a fork, go right on the road signposted main car park and ticket office. On the top of the hill to your right is the Triumphal Arch, or Arch of Hadrian. At Point **C**, turn left and rejoin Walk 33 towards the River Trent.

WHILE YOU'RE THERE

If the house itself is open, it's well worth a visit as the interior is every bit as impressive as the exterior. In addition to a fine collection of 18th-century silver, paintings and furniture, the Lichfield Display Rooms give an insight into the photographic work of Patrick Lichfield, as well as featuring an unusual display of personal memorabilia, particularly with regard to George Anson's naval exploits. Josiah Wedgwood (see Walk 28) was also a friend of the family and a number of his pieces are included in the wide range of ceramics on display.

Shelmore Great Bank

35

A short walk taking in one of the last great engineering feats of the canal-building era.

DISTANCE 2.75 miles (4.4km)	**MINIMUM TIME** 1hr
ASCENT/GRADIENT 75ft (23m) ▲▲▲	**LEVEL OF DIFFICULTY** ✦✦✦
PATHS Roads, dirt tracks and canal tow paths	
LANDSCAPE Farmland, woodland and canal	
SUGGESTED MAP OS Explorer 243 Market Drayton	
START/FINISH Grid reference: SJ 793229	
DOG FRIENDLINESS Keep on lead on road	
PARKING Roadside parking at Norbury Junction	
PUBLIC TOILETS None en route	

WALK 35 DIRECTIONS

The Shropshire Union Canal, or 'Shroppie' as it's affectionately known, runs from the edge of Wolverhampton to the Mersey at Ellesmere Port, north of Chester, a distance of about 60 miles (97km). The canal is named after the union responsible for it, which was an amalgamation of a number of local canal companies.

WHERE TO EAT AND DRINK

The Junction is a welcoming pub beside the marina. It offers bar snacks and main meals every lunchtime and evening and all day at weekends, when there's also a Sunday carvery. An outside hatch serves ice creams and the beer garden overlooks the canal. On the opposite side of the canal is the Old Wharf Tea Room, open daily all year round for snacks and hot meals.

In fact, the canal almost never got built. The Shropshire Union was originally formed with the intention of constructing railways using canal foundations, as it was believed – quite rightly as it happened – that railways were a viable alternative to canals. In the event, however, resistance to railways in Wales meant a canal was built using railway foundations, or to be more precise, the foundations of railway engineering techniques. Instead of following a river, the canal took a more direct route across country, through cuttings and on embankments, ostensibly to shorten journey times. These were major undertakings, as it was considerably more difficult to raise a wide water-tight channel 60ft (18m) above the adjoining area than it was to lay a railway line in the same place.

One embankment on the Shroppie was so problematic that it nearly scuppered the entire scheme, and it wasn't even strictly necessary. Local landowner Lord Anson refused permission for the canal to pass through his estate because he wanted to keep it unmolested for pheasant shooting, so it had to be diverted. This involved building a vast embankment over a mile (1.6km) long and 60ft (18m) higher than the surrounds.

WHILE YOU'RE THERE

At Norbury Wharf, opposite the pub, you can hire a narrow boat for a day's outing on the canal. There's also a gift shop where you can buy all manner of canal memorabilia. The Izaak Walton Cottage, 6 miles (9.7km) north-east, is also worth a visit. Walton was the author of *The Compleat Angler* (1653), the popular, and enduring, fishing book (see Walk 17). The 17th-century cottage is now a museum to his life and work. It includes a first edition of his book and is open at weekends, May to August, 1–5pm.

The man responsible for this embankment, and indeed the rest of the canal, was Thomas Telford. Today Telford is remembered more as a bridge engineer than a canal builder, counting the Menai Suspension Bridge (then the longest in the world) among his many achievements. But the Shelmore Embankment caused him more than its fair share of problems. As well as moving millions of tons of earth from the 100ft (30m) cutting at nearby Woodseaves to build it, he had to cope with collapse after collapse. In all it took six years to build the embankment alone and it was only made sound in 1835, a year after Telford's death.

The Shroppie was the last great canal to be built in Britain, but despite the increasing popularity of railways as a means of transporting raw materials and goods, it remained in use until World War One. At the beginning of the 20th century, for example, a chocolate maker by the name of Cadbury used it to pick up milk from farms between Norbury Junction and his factory at Knighton. Farmers would leave churns at collecting points along the tow path and they would then be collected and returned as empties at the end of the day.

From the car park at The Junction inn, head over the canal and bear right, following the road towards Gnosall. At the point where the road heads sharp right under the canal, go straight on up the wide gravel track that's signed for the Shelmore Trout Fishery. When this track veers right into Shelmore Wood, keep going straight along the edge of the wood, shortly coming to a gap in a high, tree-dotted hedge. Go through this gap on to a tree-lined bridleway with conifers on the left and deciduous woodland on your right. As the route becomes a concrete track opposite Norbury Park Farm, carry on along the edge of the wood as far as the Gnosall road.

WHAT TO LOOK OUT FOR

Along the edge of Shelmore Wood you might spot what look like street lamp covers lining the path; these are in fact pheasant-feeders, designed to keep the seed dry. The pheasants are hand-reared, and in winter their grain is placed in woods, where the pheasants find protection from the elements, while in spring and summer you may find feed hoppers just at the edge of the woods where the cocks establish their territories to attract the hens.

Head hard right down a short hill. At the bottom beware of cars as you walk through the tunnel (if you happen to be there when a car drives through, the noise is extraordinary). Go through a gate and up some steps to the canal.

At the top turn left to get back to the start point.

Horn Dancing in Abbots Bromley

*A colourful and ancient tradition is alive
and well in one of the county's most charming villages.*

DISTANCE 5.25 miles (8.4km)	**MINIMUM TIME** 2hrs
ASCENT/GRADIENT 525ft (160m) ▲▲▲	**LEVEL OF DIFFICULTY** +++
PATHS Roads, grass trails and gravel tracks, 16 stiles	
LANDSCAPE Farmland and village	
SUGGESTED MAP OS Explorer 244 Cannock Chase	
START/FINISH Grid reference: SK 081245	
DOG FRIENDLINESS Keep on lead at all times	
PARKING Street parking in Abbots Bromley	
PUBLIC TOILETS None en route	

The existence of Abbots Bromley can be traced back to long before the Norman Conquest of England in 1066, through a number of references in charters and wills dating from that time. The first market charter was granted in 1221 for a weekly market and an annual two-day fair to be held in the village, and this fair survives today in the form of a rare and slightly unusual ritual. One theory on the obscure origins of the horn dance is that it derived from an ancient fertility rite, another is that the dance celebrates the establishment of ancient hunting rites.

An Old Tradition

The horn dance was first performed at the Barthelmy Fair as long ago as 1226. It was originally held on the feast day of St Bartholomew, one of the apostles and the patron saint of tanners, but an alteration to the Gregorian calendar in 1752 changed this date to 4 September. Today it's held on the first weekend after the 4th, with the dance proper taking place on the Monday.

Dancing on the Village Green

According to custom six pairs of ancient reindeer horns (or more accurately antlers) are collected from St Nicholas's Church just before 8am by a small entourage of dancers comprising – among others – a fool, a hobby horse, a bowman and Maid Marion. The first dance of the day is performed on the village green with music provided by a melodion (a small reed organ similar to an accordion). Then, a tour of the nearby villages, farms and pubs ensues with the final dance taking place back at the village green. In addition to the horn dance proper, this colourful procession also features displays of morris and clog dancing. Other attractions include exhibitions and craft stalls, plus the pleasures of no fewer than five pubs in Abbots Bromley alone. Each year the dance attracts hundreds of visitors from all over the world.

As well as the horn dance, Abbots Bromley also boasts a number of other notable legends. The Goat's Head pub was once patronised by infamous highwayman Dick Turpin, who is believed to have stayed the night there after stealing a horse from Rugeley fair. And then there is the story of the Bagot goats: these black-necked beasts used to roam Bagot Woods to the north of the village and were first given to Sir John Bagot by Richard II at the end of the 14th century, in return for the hunting he enjoyed here. Legend has it that as long as the herd is maintained the Bagot family shall survive.

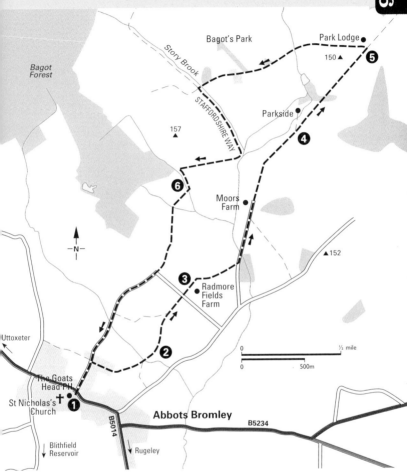

WALK 36 DIRECTIONS

1 From the Buttercross, by The Goats Head, cross the road and go up Schoolhouse Lane. At the top of the hill, turn right along Swan Lane and when you get to the end head right along a path to a stile. Head diagonally left across the field to a gap in the hedge. Go through this gap and continue across the next field to a footbridge. After the footbridge keep following the faint grassy trail to a stile near the top right-hand corner of the field.

2 Bear slightly left across the middle of the field to another stile. Carry on straight up the next field, keeping a hedge just to your left across a series of stiles and fields until you get to a road. Head

straight across the road, following
a footpath sign and, just as the
track heads hard right, go straight
on over a concrete stile and across
the next field.

3 After another stile, follow the
curve of a field to the right as far
as a metalled road. Go left here,
following the road and track as far
as Parkside farm gate. Just before
this gate, go through a gate on the
right and then left through another
series of gates.

WHAT TO LOOK OUT FOR

The wooden Buttercross
(opposite The Goats Head pub
and named after the produce
once sold under it) would have
been at the heart of the once-
thriving market and is thought
to have been built in 1339.
However, architectural historian
Nikolaus Pevsner, in *The
Buildings of England, Staffordshire*,
gives a more likely date of the
17th century.

4 Continue across the field,
with a hedge to your left, before
crossing a funnel-shaped section
of meadow to the hedge on the
far side. Follow this hedge to a stile
and wood. Bear diagonally right
through this band of trees to a pair
of footbridges and another stile.
Leaving the wood behind, head
for the far right-hand corner of
the field.

5 At the road opposite Park
Lodge turn left. Just after crossing
Story Brook head left. At the
far left-hand corner of the field,

follow the hedge round to the right
and cross a small copse. Continue
to follow the fence towards the
corner of Bagot Forest and then
go left, through the hedge. With
the hedge now on your right,
walk around the edge of the
field, swinging left, to go through
another clear gap in the hedge.

WHERE TO EAT AND DRINK

There are five different pubs
to choose from in Abbots
Bromley, which is impressive
for a large village. The Goats
Head is arguably as friendly and
welcoming as any, with timber
beams throughout and excellent
food served lunchtime and
evenings on weekdays and
all day at weekends. Bar snacks
and a variety of traditional hot
meals are available.

6 With Bagot Forest to your
right, follow the Staffordshire Way
footpath signs across the wide field
ahead, aiming for the bottom end
of a sloping hedge. When you reach
it turn left and follow its right side
up to a gate at the top of the field.
Carry on straight along the track as
far as a metalled road. Go straight
on to get back to the start.

WHILE YOU'RE THERE

Blithfield Reservoir, just to the west of Abbots Bromley, has been
designated a Site of Special Scientific Interest (SSSI) thanks to the
significant part it plays as a refuge for wildfowl and immigrant waders
such as yellow wagtails, Canada geese, great crested grebe and heron. The
shoreline at the north end of the causeway makes a very pleasant spot for
a picnic, and in the summer there is often a take-away food outlet selling
snacks, hot and cold drinks and ice creams.

Most Horrid in Rugeley

A scandalous murder trial in the 19th century brought the world's press to this quiet Staffordshire town.

DISTANCE 3.5 miles (5.7km) **MINIMUM TIME** 1hr 30min

ASCENT/GRADIENT 180ft (55m) ▲▲▲ **LEVEL OF DIFFICULTY** ✦✦✦

PATHS Roads, grass trails, tow path and gravel tracks, 8 stiles

LANDSCAPE Farmland, hilltop and canal

SUGGESTED MAP OS Explorer 244 Cannock Chase

START/FINISH Grid reference: SK 045185

DOG FRIENDLINESS Keep on lead near livestock

PARKING Side-street parking near St Augustine's Church, Rugeley

PUBLIC TOILETS None en route

Although Rugeley's existence can be traced back as far as Saxon times, today there's precious little evidence of the town's medieval past apart from the ruins of the Church of St Augustine, built in the 12th and 13th centuries. Oddly, when it needed rebuilding in the 19th century, the decision was taken to choose a new site and leave the original to the elements, with the result that the parish had two churches for the price of one.

Mysterious Deaths

Apparently, though, no amount of building to the glory of God could deliver one local character from a life of infamy. Doctor William Palmer, the son of a timber merchant, married Ann Brooks in 1847. She subsequently bore him five children, but four died mysteriously in infancy. Ann's father also died under suspicious circumstances and, when her grieving mother came to stay, she too was dead within the space of a week.

Later, when William owed money to a bookmaker, the bookie suddenly became very ill and died before he had a chance to collect his cash. In the meantime, William took out insurance policies for his wife and brother, but they both died soon after the first payments had been made. The insurance company refused to pay out, so – heavily in debt – William went to the races with a friend by the name of John Parsons Cook. As luck would have it, Cook won, but unfortunately died before picking up his winnings. So who do you suppose showed up to collect them? Why, Dr William Palmer of course!

Murder Most Foul

By this stage, it wasn't just the insurance company who were crying foul, and Palmer was arrested for Cook's murder. The newspapers of the time called it the 'Trial of the Century' and for weeks it was headline news. After over a month in court Palmer was eventually found guilty and was publicly executed in Stafford at 8am on Saturday 14 June 1856, in front of a crowd of 10,000. But that wasn't the end of William Palmer. So notorious were his crimes, and so voracious was the press in reporting them, that his name, at least, endured for more than 100 years, as a waxwork model in Madame Tussaud's Chamber of Horrors. Remarkably, it stayed there until 1979.

Such was the press coverage of the trial that rumours were rife. One apocryphal story tells how the people of Rugeley were so horrified by the scandal surrounding the trial that they petitioned Parliament to have the name of the town changed. The story goes that the Prime Minister considered the petition and agreed the town name could only be changed if they named it after him; the problem was, his named was Palmerston.

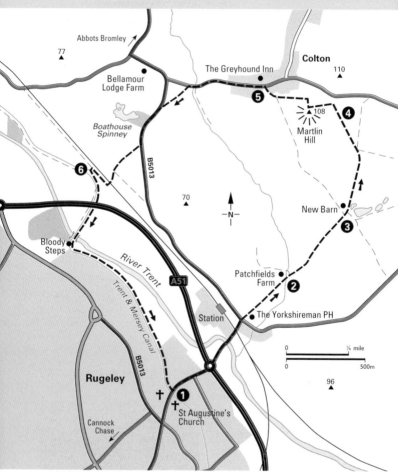

WALK 37 DIRECTIONS

1 From St Augustine's Church head right along the B5013 towards Abbots Bromley. After going over two roundabouts, the river and under the railway, continue straight on along the track just to the left of The

Yorkshireman pub. When you get to Parchfields Farm, go over a stile on the right and across a field to a pair of stiles and a footbridge.

2 Cross the footbridge and head diagonally left across the field to its far corner. Head over a stile here and straight along the right-

WHERE TO EAT AND DRINK

The Greyhound Inn in Colton is a friendly and charming pub, serving a range of snacks and traditional main meals most evenings and at Sunday lunchtimes. The pub's open 5:30–11pm every weekday and noon until close at weekends.

hand edge of the field, keeping the hedge just to your right. At the end of the field, follow the yellow footpath arrows right and then left and continue in the same direction to New Barn.

3 At the track T-junction just beyond New Barn, head left past the house and keep on this track, bearing slightly right, along the edge of the field, keeping the hedge to your right-hand side. The hedge curves round to the left and, after a further 150yds (137m), go through the gate in the top right-hand corner of the field. Continue in the same direction, again keeping the hedge to the right, until you get to the top of this field.

WHILE YOU'RE THERE

Nearby Cannock Chase offers some of the best mountain biking in the Midlands. With miles of wide gravel track and lots of free parking, it's ideal for both a short potter and an all-day epic. There's a bike centre and hire shop at Birches Valley Visitors' Centre just west of Rugeley (see Walks 38–40).

4 Head left here for about 100yds (91m) to a stile in the fence. Cross the stile and follow this fence as it goes left to the top of the Martlin Hill. At the summit turn 90 degrees to the right and follow the fence down to a stile on the left. Go over and head downhill to a stile in the bottom right corner. Go over another stile and join a short track into Colton.

5 Go left through the village and, just after the road bears right after a small bridge, go left along a footpath that diagonally crosses a field. Follow this footpath until it brings you out on to the B5013 and then go left for 150yds (137m). Just after the road bears left, head right, down a wide gravel track and cross over the railway line before turning hard right for another 150yds (137m) to reach the canal.

6 Without crossing the bridge, head left along the canal tow path and follow this all the way to the B5013. Just before you reach the bridge go up a ramp and then right, back to the start.

WHAT TO LOOK OUT FOR

Just after the canal crosses the river towards the end of the walk, you should be able to see the tow path on the far side of the canal leading to some steps. These steps were the scene of another infamous crime, when a woman named Christina Collins was murdered by three men in 1839. When they were caught, one was hung, one was deported to Australia and the third was sent to prison. Christina's body was buried at the new St Augustine's Church.

Cannock's Memorials

This heathland walk serves as a poignant reminder of less peaceful times.

DISTANCE 4 miles (6.4km)	**MINIMUM TIME** 1hr 30min
ASCENT/GRADIENT 361ft (110m) ▲▲▲	**LEVEL OF DIFFICULTY** ✦✦✦
PATHS Gravel tracks, dirt paths and roads	
LANDSCAPE Heather and woodland	
SUGGESTED MAP OS Explorer 244 Cannock Chase	
START/FINISH Grid reference: SJ 980181	
DOG FRIENDLINESS Beware of cyclists at all times	
PARKING Ample parking at start point	
PUBLIC TOILETS None en route	

At the beginning of the 20th century Cannock Chase was very different from the way it is now, due to centuries of deforestation. A long history of iron smelting and the consequent demand for charcoal and then coal had left the landscape almost treeless.

Army Training Camp

But the bleak landscape reflected bleaker times. With the outbreak of World War I, the Chase seemed like the perfect place for an army training camp and, between 1914 and 1918, 250,000 British and Commonwealth troops passed through here on their way to the trenches. Many would not return.

The camp occupied much of the area covered by this walk. There were training areas and firing ranges and also a railway, sewage works, a prisoner of war camp, a powerhouse and pumping station, and quarters for troops and officers. Equally important were the veterinary hospital at Chase Road Corner (horses were still a large part of military life) and the Great War Hospital at Brindley Heath, for wounded soldiers brought back from the front.

Many German, British and Commonwealth soldiers who died in the War Hospital were buried in the Commonwealth Cemetery, which today is a quiet, contemplative, immaculately preserved place. Equally moving is the German War Cemetery, just to the north-east. It was established by the German War Graves Commission, an organisation charged with caring for the graves of victims of war and tyranny. The commission was asked by the German government to take care of over 1.4 million graves, in 343 cemeteries throughout 24 different countries.

After the German-British War Graves Treaty of 1959, most of the German soldiers in cemeteries around Britain were exhumed and transferred to the cemetery at Cannock Chase, and today it is the only German war cemetery in the UK. It is the final resting place for 2,143 servicemen who died in World War I and 2,797 who died in World War II. In all, 1,307 Germans remain in other British cemeteries (including the Commonwealth Cemetery here) and are looked after by the Commonwealth War Graves Commission. Read the poem on the wall of the visitor centre; it says it all.

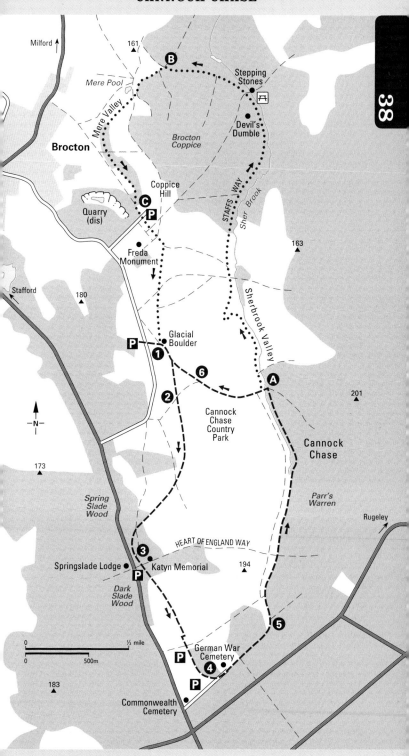

Milford

161

B

Mere Pool

Stepping
Stones

Mere Valley

Devil's
Dumble

Brocton

Brocton
Coppice

Coppice
Hill

STAFFS WAY

Sher Brook

C
P

Quarry
(dis)

Freda
Monument

163

Stafford

180

Sherbrook Valley

P

1

Glacial
Boulder

6

2

A

201

Cannock
Chase
Country Park

Cannock
Chase

Parr's
Warren

–N–

Rugeley

173

Spring
Slade
Wood

HEART OF ENGLAND WAY

3

Springslade Lodge

Katyn Memorial

P

194

Dark
Slade
Wood

5

0   ½ mile

0   500m

P

German War
Cemetery

183

4

P

Commonwealth
Cemetery

WALK 38 DIRECTIONS

❶ From the Glacial Boulder, walk away from the road along a narrow path past the trig point and then turn right along the wide gravel track. When you get to a fork, go right, following the Heart of England Way footpath sign.

WHAT TO LOOK OUT FOR

To the right of the visitor centre are the massive grave stones marking the deaths of four Zeppelin crews shot down over England in World War I. They were originally buried in Potters Bar, Burstead and Theberton. Much harder to find are the graves of the 90 unknown soldiers buried here; one near to the centre is marked simply: 'Zwei unbekannte Deutsche Soldaten.'

❷ At a crossroads of paths, continue in the same direction (ignoring a footpath off to the right). At the next path junction, again carry straight on as the path curves gradually around the right. Continue along this track across several more path crossroads until your path curves round to the left alongside the road. At the point where another wide track comes in from the left, go straight on rather than taking the shortcut down to the road.

❸ After crossing the narrow surfaced road opposite Springslade Lodge, continue up a dirt track and across a path crossroads. After about 500yds (457m), you come to a T-junction in the path which requires a dog-leg right then left to keep going in the same direction through a car park. Continue in this direction to a second car park and, as the track curves around to the left, another metalled road.

❹ Turn left past the German War Cemetery until the road becomes a wide gravel track. Continue along this track, down into the woods, and when you get to the fork go left down the hill.

❺ Continue along the bottom of the valley for a mile (1.6km), staying to the right of the stream and ignoring all paths off, until you get to the obvious ford where the conifers end. Cross the stream using the stepping stones. At the junction on the other side, head away from the stream following a track left around the bottom of a hill ahead, rather than right, straight over the top of it. Follow this track as it curves round to the right, all the way to the top of the hill.

WHERE TO EAT AND DRINK

Springslade Lodge is a great place to stop for refreshments in the summer, with plenty of outside seating, but its indoor tea room is also popular in the winter (closed on Mondays and Fridays, October to March). It offers a range of hot snacks, as well as tasty main meals.

❻ Continue across the plateau until the path starts to descend the other side, at which point you rejoin the path, heading right, back towards the start and the car park.

WHILE YOU'RE THERE

The Katyn Memorial, just a short walk from Springslade Lodge, is a tribute to the 14,000 members of the Polish armed forces and professional classes executed in 1940 in Katyn Forest, near Smolensk, by the Soviet secret police on the orders of Stalin. The Poles had been prisoners of war following the Soviet Union's invasion of Poland while Germany was invading from the west; another 7,000 who were shot have never been found.

Coppice Hill and the Freda Memorial

Extend the walk to take in more of the former military training ground.
See map and information panel for Walk 38

DISTANCE *7 miles (11.3km)* **MINIMUM TIME** *2hrs 30min*

ASCENT/GRADIENT *361ft (110m)* ▲▲▲ **LEVEL OF DIFFICULTY** ✦✦✦

WALK 39 DIRECTIONS
(Walk 38 option)

After crossing the stream at Point **A**, head right along the Sherbrook Valley, following the stream until it joins the Staffordshire Way. Continue along the stream as far as Devil's Dumble and the picnic site at Stepping Stones. Don't cross the stream, but carry on past the ford

WHAT TO LOOK OUT FOR
The area around Mere Pool used to be the camp sewage works and sludge beds. The path along the side of Mere Valley beyond the pools was a part of the camp railway which connected with the station in Milford a mile (1.6km) or so to the north. The Glacial Boulder stands on the base of what was once the camp reservoir tower. The boulder itself is granite, and has been identified as originating in Scotland. It was scoured out by glaciers during the last ice age and deposited near by.

until you get to a T-junction in the tracks, Point **B**. Head left here, leaving the Staffordshire Way, and follow signs for Mere Pool.

At the next major path junction, at Mere Pool, turn hard left almost back on yourself, following signs for the Heart of England Way towards Coppice Hill. Carry on along Mere Valley, ignoring any paths off to the left or right, and follow the track round to the left up Hollywood Slade. At a metalled road, Point **C**, bear slightly left to cross the road and then continue in the same direction as before.

After 250yds (229m) take the right fork, still following the Heart of England Way. Go across the next diagonal crosspaths and continue the final 400yds (366m) to the start.

WHILE YOU'RE THERE
About 200yds (183m) after Point **C**, head right along a grass trail for 150yds (137m) to see the monument to Freda, canine mascot of the New Zealand Rifle Brigade. Freda was a Dalmatian adopted by the brigade when they were camped at Cannock Chase and it's thought that she accompanied them to the Battle of the Somme in 1916. Today, more than 70 New Zealand soldiers are buried at the Commonwealth Cemetery, while Freda was buried at Cannock Chase in 1918. Her collar, bearing the inscription 'Freda of the NZ Rifle Brigade', is kept in the Army Museum at Waiouru, New Zealand.

Burning Cannock Chase

Explore an Area of Outstanding Natural Beauty once ravaged by industry.

40

DISTANCE 3.5 miles (5.7km)   **MINIMUM TIME** 1hr 15min

ASCENT/GRADIENT 270ft (82m) ▲▲▲   **LEVEL OF DIFFICULTY** ✦✦✦

PATHS Gravel tracks

LANDSCAPE Forest and forest pools

SUGGESTED MAP OS Explorer 244 Cannock Chase

START/FINISH Grid reference: SK 018172

DOG FRIENDLINESS Can be off lead, but beware of bikes

PARKING Birches Valley Forest Centre pay car park

PUBLIC TOILETS At Forest Centre at start

WALK 40 DIRECTIONS

Cannock Chase, a vast area of open heathland and conifer forest just to the north of Birmingham, has been the site of human activity for thousands of years. Prehistoric hunter-gatherers built massive earthworks here (see While You're There), and William the Conqueror, realising that the heavily forested area would be difficult to cultivate, declared it a royal hunting forest. As a result, anyone caught killing a small animal lost an eye or one hand, while anyone caught poaching deer was executed.

While many other forests were exploited for wood in the centuries that followed, the precedent set by William I protected the chase from deforestation and it remained a hunting forest until Tudor times. Under the reign of Henry VIII, however, the title to the chase was given to William Paget, later the Marquis of Anglesey, who secured a licence to fell trees for iron smelting in 1560. Today, Marquis's Drive, running more or less right across the chase, is a reminder of his legacy, but it was his deeds rather than his name that had the greatest impact on the landscape.

Iron smelting relied on vast quantities of charcoal to fire early blast furnaces. With the help of water-powered bellows, a mixture of charcoal, limestone and cinders was used to melt the iron ore, which was subsequently poured into troughs as cast iron, an alloy of carbon and iron. This mixture was very brittle, so even more charcoal was required to burn off the carbon so that it could finally be hammered into wrought iron. The bars of iron produced in this way were then heated a final time, to be rolled flat and slit by a water-powered mill. By the end of the 16th century, the process was

---

WHERE TO EAT AND DRINK

The Birches Valley Café at the Forest Centre is open daily throughout the year and sells an array of snacks and refreshments, including sandwiches, salads, jacket potatoes, soup and speciality coffees.

CANNOCK CHASE

refined enough to produce items like nails, locks and chains. But the new technology came at a price and by 1610, Cannock Chase had been almost completely deforested by voracious charcoal-burners.

It was still treeless 240 years later when the Cannock Chase Colliery came into being. The area was first mined for coal in 1298 but it wasn't until the height of the Industrial Revolution that it became big business. With coal came people, and the increase in population soon pushed back the boundaries of the remaining green areas further still.

Mining continued well into the 20th century, and it wasn't until the 1920s and 30s that trees began to be systematically replanted in the area. By the end of World War II, coal mining was confined to larger pits, and many of the smaller pits were closed. In 1958 much of the woodland and heather was declared an Area of Outstanding Natural Beauty (AONB), and since then most of it has returned back to nature.

From the car park at the Birches Valley Forest Centre, go left along Penkridge Bank (metalled road) and, after 200yds (183m), turn left along a wide gravel bridleway.

Stay left on the main track here, avoiding a less obvious grass track up the hill to the right.

At a path junction just before Stony Brook, go right along the wide bridleway. Shortly after, you come to a fork. Stay left, following a track alongside Stonybrook Pools and Fairoak Pools.

When you get to a main intersection of two bridleways, about 200yds (183m) beyond the last main pool, head left. Keep on the main gravel track, ignoring routes off ahead and left and instead swing up right, into the trees.

Continue to the far end of the path, then turn left along Marquis's Drive (metalled, pedestrian only road). Pass the large wooden sign to Hednesford on the right and carry on for another 300yds (274m) until the now unsurfaced road curves gently left.

Soon after, go left down a signposted bridleway that soon dips downhill between the rows of conifers. Ignore paths off left and right and continue down the long, straight track. At the crossroads at the bottom of the hill go left along another wide gravel bridleway to Stony Brook. Cross the stream and retrace your footsteps back to the car park.

What the Romans Did for Brewood

A walk skirting a reservoir and taking in the intersection of two remarkable feats of engineering.

41

DISTANCE 5.75 miles (9.2km)   **MINIMUM TIME** 2hrs

ASCENT/GRADIENT 75ft (23m) ▲▲▲   **LEVEL OF DIFFICULTY** ✦✦✦

PATHS Tow paths, grass trails and roads, 3 stiles

LANDSCAPE Canal, farmland and reservoir

SUGGESTED MAP OS Explorer 242 Telford, Ironbridge & The Wrekin

START/FINISH Grid reference: SJ 881088

DOG FRIENDLINESS Must be kept on lead near livestock

PARKING Ample side-street parking in Brewood

PUBLIC TOILETS None en route

The first thing you need to know about Brewood is that it's pronounced 'brood', and getting this right first time round will instantly endear you to locals. The name, cited as Breude in the Domesday Book (1086), is a hybrid word from the Celtic 'bre', or hill, and the Old English 'wuda', meaning wood.

Roman Roads

It was during the Roman occupation of Britain that the area to the north of Brewood was first established as a main transport route, for it was here that Watling Street was built, stretching from London (Londinium) all the way to present-day Wroxeter, just to the west of Shrewsbury. It was just one of the dozens of major roads built by the Romans across Britain, the longest of which were Fosse Way (from Exeter to Lincoln), Ermine Street (from London to York) and of course Watling Street, built in the first years of the invasion (AD 100), and later extended to Chester.

Built to Last

Roman roads in Britain were an extension of a systematic network connecting Rome to the four corners of its vast empire, built principally as a means of moving its great armies quickly and efficiently across occupied countries. In order to do this they had to be exceptionally well constructed. They were usually built on a raised embankment (to allow adequate drainage), made out of rubble obtained from drainage ditches built on either side. Next came the layer of sand, or gravel and sand, sometimes mixed with clay; and finally the whole thing was metalled with flint, finer gravel or even the slag from the smelting of iron. The finished road was often several feet thick, cambered to allow water to run off it and with kerb stones on each side to channel any excess water.

Given the complexity of the roads, the huge distances covered and the realisation that every single inch was laboriously built by hand, the fact that many Roman roads – or at least their foundations – still exist today provides mute testimony to the mind-boggling efforts of their builders.

Opposite: Fairoak Pools, Cannock Chase at sunset (Walk 40)

BREWOOD

In addition to being well designed and well maintained, however, Roman roads also invariably followed straight lines. Today's A5 follows the route of Watling Street for much of its length, and you only have to glance at an atlas to see how much straighter it is than any modern road. This was achieved by lining up marker posts and the result meant both faster journey times and a much more efficient communications network.

It's worth noting that the Shropshire Union Canal, which bisects Watling Street just to the north of Brewood, was built along similar principles, raised on great embankments and built in a series of straight lines, ultimately to improve travel times (see Walk 35).

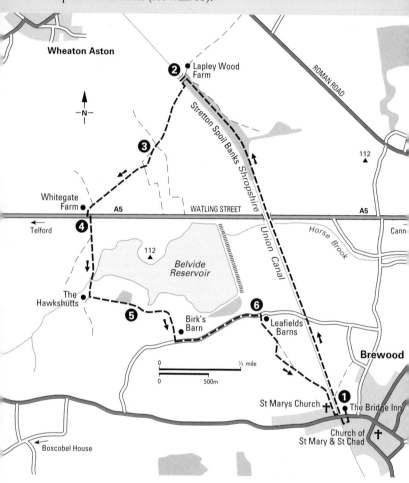

WALK 41 DIRECTIONS

❶ From The Bridge Inn car park, go straight across the main road and down some steps to the canal. Go right at the bottom of the steps and follow the canal tow path as far as the A5 and then through

Stretton Spoil Banks to Bridge No 17 near Lapley Wood Farm.

❷ Cross over the bridge and, at the concrete track, turn left for 100yds (91m). Just as this track bears right, go through the gate in the hedge to your right. Follow the hedge along the edge of the field and then along a dirt trail through a thin strip of woodland.

3 At the end of the trees, go through the gate directly ahead and then diagonally left across a field to its left-hand corner. Go through another gate and continue in the same direction along the left-hand edge of the field. At the end of this long field go through the gate and across another small field to the edge of Whitegate Farm.

4 Skirt round the left-hand edge of the courtyard to reach the gate on to the A5. Take care crossing this busy main road and then head left for 50yds (46m) before turning right along the metalled farm road. Follow this as far as The Hawkshutts and, opposite the farmhouse, go left through a gate and head straight across the field, past the right-hand corner of the wood ahead, and across the next field to a gate ahead.

5 After going through the gate, bear right along a path through bushes and trees as far as the gate into another field. Bear slightly left here, aiming for the middle of the

41

trees ahead, until you get to a gate and a gravel-surfaced farm track. Go right, along this track and then bear left along the road after Birk's Barn, following it as far as Leafields Barns.

6 Go over a stile on the right, then after a second beyond a driveway go diagonally left across a field in the direction of the church steeples until you get to a stile. Cross the stile and head right, around the edge of the field, to a line of trees down the middle. Head left here, following the line of trees as far as a gravel track. Go ahead up the track to the canal and then turn right, back towards St Mary's Church and the start.

Lichfield's Soaring Heaven on Earth

A short and relatively simple town walk exploring the impact of the county's most magnificent cathedral.

DISTANCE 2.5 miles (4km) **MINIMUM TIME** 1hr

ASCENT/GRADIENT Negligible ▲▲▲ **LEVEL OF DIFFICULTY** ✦✦✦

PATHS Roads, surfaced paths and dirt trails

LANDSCAPE Town centre and parkland

SUGGESTED MAP OS Explorers 232 Nuneaton & Tamworth; 244 Cannock Chase

START/FINISH Grid reference: SK 118095 (on Explorer 232)

DOG FRIENDLINESS Must be kept on lead near roads

PARKING Ample paid parking in Lichfield town centre

PUBLIC TOILETS Town centre locations and Beacon Park

The story of Lichfield begins soon after the death of Christ. In about AD 300, during the reign of Roman Emperor Diocletian, 1,000 Christians were martyred in this area. The name Lichfield, which literally means 'field of the dead', commemorates the event. As a martyr shrine, it soon became a centre of Christianity and, in AD 669, the Bishop of Mercia, Chad, established his seat here. Although Chad was only a bishop for three years, such was his zeal and holiness that he converted many to Christianity.

Gothic Cathedral
When Chad died in AD 672, he was buried close to the existing Church of St Mary. It wasn't long before his shrine became known as a place for miracles and in AD 700, a new church dedicated to St Peter was built to receive his body. Later, a Norman cathedral was built on the same site, but a new Gothic cathedral was begun in 1085, this time dedicated to St Chad. Finally, after 150 years, the greatest cathedral in all the land was finished…

Place of Pilgrimage
Imagine you're a peasant living near Lichfield when the cathedral is first completed. You might have a small wattle and daub (wood and mud) house, some leather jerkins and sackcloth shoes. You might have seen a small Saxon or Norman church before, but more likely, if you live out in the country, you've never seen a stone building in your life, let alone one higher than two storeys.

Soaring Spires
You hear people talking about a new church being constructed in nearby Lichfield. They say it's constructed of stone and reaches up to the heavens, but nothing you've heard can prepare you for the sheer scale of what you find when you make your pilgrimage, on foot, to this new house of God. No fewer than three gigantic spires soar into the sky and when you get close,

Opposite: Lichfield Cathedral from Pool Walk (Walk 42)

approaching the vast west façade, it's so big that it feels like it's falling on top of you (try this as you're walking up to it yourself).

Gold and Silver

The cathedral as we see it today has hardly changed from the one exalted by Christian pilgrims and peasants some 800 years ago. If anything, it would probably have been more impressive in those times. Much of the stonework would have been painted silver and gold and the interior would have been more foreboding, lit only by the much darker stained-glass windows of medieval times. Most of the stained glass in the cathedral today dates from the 19th century and is much lighter.

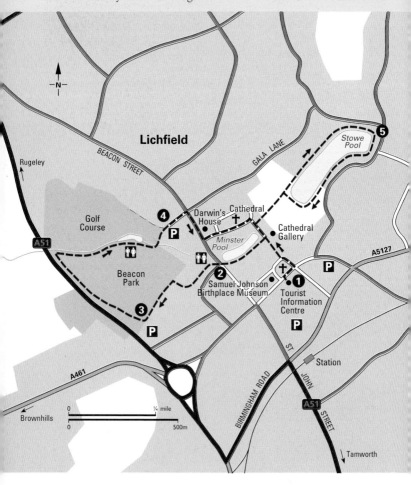

WALK 42 DIRECTIONS

❶ From the tourist information centre, next to the Garrick theatre, go through Three Spires shopping arcade and turn left on to Conduit Street and ahead to Market Square. Carry straight along Dam Street, past a series of tea shops and cafés, until you get to Pool Walk. Go left here, keeping Minster Pool on your right-hand side, until you get to Beacon Street.

WHERE TO EAT AND DRINK

Chapters Coffee Shop is the ideal spot to stop for morning coffee, Sunday lunch or afternoon tea. It has a wide variety of snacks, meals and traditional English desserts and a welcoming and relaxed setting right across from the cathedral.

2 Go diagonally right over Beacon Street to the public toilets and the entrance to the park. Skirt around the left-hand edge of the park, keeping first the bowling lawn and then the tennis courts to your right. After the tennis courts follow a path round to the right and, at the next path junction, walk left, continuing around the edge of the park.

3 When you get to the car park bear slightly right, following the path to the far end of the playing fields. After the path has entered the narrow band of trees, and just before the A51, turn right along a narrow dirt trail and carry on to the golf course at the far end. Just before the footbridge on to the golf course, turn right and follow the small brook back along the edge of the playing fields until you reach a small lake. In the summer it's possible to hire boats here for

WHILE YOU'RE THERE

Lichfield is a pretty market town with great shopping and plenty to see. Among the highlights are the Samuel Johnson Birthplace Museum, commemorating the life and work of the celebrated writer who, along with a number of famous sayings, was responsible for the first comprehensive English dictionary. Also worth visiting is the house of Erasmus Darwin (1731–1802), the grandfather of Charles Darwin, who was a brilliant doctor, scientist, inventor and poet.

a potter on the water. Continue on past the lake before crossing over a footbridge to the left to reach Shaw Lane.

WHAT TO LOOK OUT FOR

The Cathedral's chapter house boasts the so-called Lichfield Gospels, an illuminated Latin manuscript dating from the 8th century. It's hard to imagine that the elaborately decorated pages of this ancient book were written, painted and bound more than 1,200 years ago. The Chapel of St Michael is where the campaigns of the Staffordshire Regiment are commemorated. It also contains a book of remembrance with names of the men who fell in the world wars (see Walk 43).

4 Follow Shaw Lane until you get to Beacon Street, then go right for 150yds (137m) and then left along The Close to reach the cathedral. If you're not in any rush, it's worth doing a quick circuit of the cathedral inside and out, before continuing. There's an excellent shop with leaflets and guides and a free leaflet is also available, which describes the cathedral's highlights. Bear to the right of the cathedral and, at the end of The Close, just after Chapters Coffee Shop, go right down Dam Street and then immediately left down Reeve Lane to Stowe Pool. From the far end of Stowe Pool you can look back at the cathedral's towers and see right through the windows from one side to the other, giving the impression that they're lighter and more delicate than stone.

5 Continue on the popular surfaced path all the way round the edge of Stowe Pool and return to Dam Street, before retracing your steps to the tourist information centre at the start.

A Walk to Whittington's Victoria Cross

A gentle walk taking in the history of Britain's most distinguished medal.

43

DISTANCE 6.75 miles (10.9km)   **MINIMUM TIME** 2hrs 30min

ASCENT/GRADIENT 180ft (55m) ▲▲▲   **LEVEL OF DIFFICULTY** +++

PATHS Roads, gravel and sand tracks, dirt trails, may be muddy after rain, 2 stiles

LANDSCAPE Farmland and forest

SUGGESTED MAP OS Explorer 232 Nuneaton & Tamworth

START/FINISH Grid reference: SK 158083

DOG FRIENDLINESS On lead near livestock and roads

PARKING Ample roadside parking in Whittington

PUBLIC TOILETS None en route

NOTE At the time of writing the military firing range is not in use, but if firing recommences Hopwas Hays Lane will be subject to temporary closures

---

Whittington Barracks, just south of the village of the same name, has been the home of the Staffordshire Regiment since 1881. The regiment's origins date back to 1705, when the 38th Foot was raised at the King's Head Hotel in Lichfield by Colonel Luke Lillingston, and it first saw active service fighting the French and Spanish in the West Indies. The raising of other regiments over the next 120 years led, through a complex process of change and reorganisation, to the formation of the Staffordshire Regiment after the end of World War II and its recent amalgamation into the Mercian Regiment. It was conferred the title of the Prince of Wales's in 1876, following the presentation of colours by the Prince of Wales (later crowned King Edward VII). Today, its Colonel in Chief is HRH the Duke of York, Prince Andrew.

All of this history, and much more besides, is related by the fascinating Staffordshire Regiment Museum at Whittington Barracks, with a chronological display of information and memorabilia from the many campaigns the regiment has been embroiled in. The most interesting of these displays, however, is arguably the one dedicated to the story of the Victoria Cross, and to those in the regiment who have been awarded this, the highest wartime honour.

Acts of Valour

The Victoria Cross was first established by royal warrant in 1856, to recognise acts of uncommon valour during the Crimean War, 1854–56. It was ordained that it should 'only be awarded for most conspicuous bravery, or some daring or pre-eminent act of valour or self-sacrifice or extreme devotion to duty in the presence of the enemy.' Each VC is forged from the remains of two Russian cannon, captured at Sebastopol, the last great battle of the Crimean War. The metal itself is guarded by 15 Regiment in Donnington, secured in vaults and rarely removed; the most recent issue of metal, sufficient to make 12 medals, was made in 1959. It's thought the remaining metal is enough to make a further 85 medals; given that only 11 have been won since the end of World War II, it can only be hoped that this will suffice for many years to come.

In all, 1,354 Victoria Crosses have been won, and of these, 1,156 were awarded before the end of World War I. At least three witnesses are needed for recommendation. All medals require royal assent and are presented by the reigning monarch. The inscription on front of the VC states simply: 'For Valour'. It has been estimated that the chances of surviving a VC action is 1 in 10.

Lance Corporal William Coltman

Of the 11 members of the Staffordshire Regiment who have been awarded the VC, probably the most famous is Lance Corporal William Coltman, a stretcher bearer during operations at Mannequin Hill in France on 3 and 4 October 1918. Hearing that wounded men had been left behind during a retreat, Corporal Coltman went forward alone in the face of relentless enemy fire, found the casualties, dressed their wounds and carried some of them to safety on his back on three occasions. For the next two days and nights he looked after the wounded constantly. He later became the most decorated NCO of World War I.

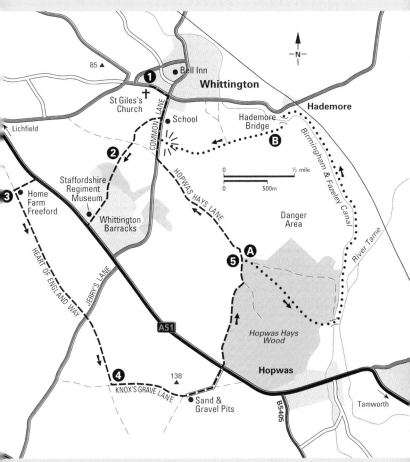

WALK 43 DIRECTIONS

43

❶ From St Giles's Church go right to the crossroads and then right for 250yds (229m) until you get to Sandy Lane. Follow this wide gravel track until it goes hard right, and here go ahead through a gate and continue in the same direction to the corner of a wood.

❷ Go through a swing gate and carry straight on ahead/left, following the direction of the yellow public footpath arrow. At the residential tarmac road bear left, as far as a main road, and then right all the way up to the Staffordshire Regiment Museum. Turn right and walk along the pavement of the A51 for 700yds (640m). At South Lodge turn left for a bridleway to Home Farm Freeford.

❸ Turn left and follow the Heart of England Way for one mile (1.6km). Cross a metalled road then go past a small square of trees on the right and keep going straight over a farm track. Another 500yds (457m) brings you to a junction with Knox's Grave Lane, a wide sandy track.

❹ Go left along here and then fork right at the top of a field to reach the corner of the sand and gravel pits. Thread between the pits on either side and keep going

along the surfaced road, down the dip and then up the other side. At the top of the rise, cross the stile on the left and head diagonally left across the field on the faint grass track. At the far side of the field, cross a stile and the A51 and then go straight up the track to a T-junction. Go left and follow the edge of Hopwas Hays Wood for 0.5 mile (800m).

❺ At a 4-way path junction go left down to the corner of the wood. From here follow the track of Hopwas Hays Lane for another 0.5 mile (800m). At the fork in the track head right, across the firing range and back down to Common Lane. Go right here, back towards Whittington and, at the crossroads, turn left to return to the start.

Hopwas Hays Wood

Extend your walk to the Birmingham and Fazeley Canal towpath.
See map and information panel for Walk 43

44

DISTANCE *9 miles (14.5km)* **MINIMUM TIME** *3hrs 30min*

ASCENT/GRADIENT *300ft (91m)* ▲▲▲ **LEVEL OF DIFFICULTY** +++

NOTE *Firing range restrictions may apply, see note on Walk 43*

WALK 44 DIRECTIONS
(Walk 43 option)

At Point **Ⓐ**, head hard right at the major 4-way junction, almost back on yourself, for a slightly sunken track through the woodland. After about 150yds (137m) head right at another fork and stay straight along this wide dirt and gravel track, ignoring any smaller paths off to the left or right. As the path starts to drop down through the woods to the canal, just keep following it round to the left as far as the bridge.

Cross over the canal and turn left along the tow path for 1.75 miles (2.8km) until 50 yards (46m) beyond Hademore House Bridge turn back right for a bridleway over the canal. Cross the bridge and continue straight ahead along a wide, sand track for 150yds (137m) and then go right along another sand track as far as a gap in the hedge ahead, Point **Ⓑ**.

Go through the gap and continue in the same direction, following a path until it goes between two hedges along a narrow dirt trail. At a T-junction with a wide track, head left and then immediately right, along another narrow dirt trail to the right of a hedge.

Beyond an iron gate and a military firing range sign (see What To Look Out For, if red flags are flying), follow the footpath sign right along the faint grass trail around the edge of the field, keeping the hedge on your right. Carry on to the far right-hand corner of this field where the hedge meets a small cottage and the metalled road (Common Lane) back into Whittington.

WHAT TO LOOK OUT FOR

If the red flags are flying, keep out! The area around Hopwas Hays Wood, marked by red triangles on OS maps, is a military firing range open to the public when it's not in use. Towards the end of the extension, just before you get to Common Lane, if you look back over your left shoulder you'll see just such a range stretching 800yds (732m) to the target area at the far end. If that doesn't sound like a long way to shoot a high-powered rifle, try to imagine hitting a target smaller than a bus from this distance, while bearing in mind that sharp shooters can group six shots in an area smaller than a playing card.

Chasewater Conservation

A walk through a country park, now a haven for watersports and wildlife.

DISTANCE 3 miles (4.8km)	**MINIMUM TIME** 1hr
ASCENT/GRADIENT 75ft (23m) ▲▲▲	**LEVEL OF DIFFICULTY** ✦✦✦

PATHS Gravel tracks

LANDSCAPE Lakeside and heathland

SUGGESTED MAP OS Explorer 244 Cannock Chase

START/FINISH Grid reference: SK 040071

DOG FRIENDLINESS Can be taken off lead

PARKING Ample parking at start point

PUBLIC TOILETS At visitor centre

WALK 45 DIRECTIONS

Originally Chasewater was a natural reservoir called Norton Pool, but little is known about its history prior to the late 18th century; with its poor acidic soil, heathland and forest, it was unsuitable for cultivation. But during the Napoleonic Wars (1803–15) there was a drive throughout the country to increase food production for troops at the front, so many previously uncultivated areas of heathland and forest were farmed.

In 1797, a dam was constructed to turn it into a feeder reservoir for the new Anglesey Branch Canal, built to carry coal from local pits to Birmingham and beyond. A steam-driven pump lifted water back into the reservoir from the canal, as it had a very small natural catchment area (only the valve house remains today, on top of the dam wall).

With the arrival of the railways in the second half of the 19th century however, canals were – quite literally – overtaken by the new technology. A network of tracks was soon established in the area, including a causeway across the water which carried coal from Cannock Chase. Mining in the area around Chasewater continued well into the 20th century, but by 1950 it was an industry in decline, leaving behind a desolate landscape littered with disused railways, sidings and pit waste.

WHERE TO EAT AND DRINK

The South Shore Café, adjoining the Chasewater Innovation Centre, is open daily, all year round. It serves a range of snacks and light refreshments, including freshly made sandwiches and a salad bar. In the summer, you can take an ice cream out onto the waterfront.

Even back then, though, the local authority had the foresight to transform Chasewater into an aquatic pleasure park, complete with funfair, big wheel and miniature railway. The funfair is no more, but the park has recently undergone renovation and now features a waterskiing centre, as well as sailing, wind surfing and a number of other water-based sports. For those who prefer their leisure pursuits a little more… well, leisurely, there are displays and interpretation at Chasewater Innovation Centre (free admission, open daily, all year).

But of course, all this has little to do with the thriving wildlife of this park, which is arguably the most significant achievement of the reclamation programme. It comprises three main habitats: waterside, heathland and bog.

Because water levels rise in the winter and fall in the summer, the sediment along the shore when the water is low (the littoral zone) makes an ideal feeding ground for wading birds like heron, pied wagtail and ringed plover. The stringy mat of weed over the exposed beaches is the rare but aptly named shoreweed. During winter, the water becomes more important than the shore for many birds, particularly coot, mute swans and a vast roost of gulls, best watched from the south shore in late afternoon. Cormorants and Canada geese are also common and great crested grebes can often be spotted displaying in spring. In all, some 230 different species have been spotted here.

Heathland favours plants that thrive in acid conditions: areas that have been reclaimed from mining activities tend to support only coarse grasses and support little in the way of wildlife. Naturally formed grassland, though, boasts a rich variety of plants such as lichens, mosses and cowslips. Finally, boggy areas can be divided into two types: true bog, which supports sphagnum moss and acid-loving plants like cotton grass, and fen, which is alkaline and harbours reed mace and marsh orchids. Today, much of the area has been designated as a Site of Special Scientific Interest (SSSI).

From the car park, go past the Innovation Centre and adjoining café and down to the shore of the reservoir and turn right. Walk across the concrete embankment and then go right, off the path, following the road round to the left, towards Chasewater Sailing Club.

Where the road turns hard left, carry straight on along a wide gravel track, following the cycle route signs. Keep following this track around, ignoring a path to the left, then forking left before the road. Go past some sports pitches to reach Chasewater Heaths Station.

Stay on the main track as it veers left, back towards the reservoir, as far as the railway embankment.

Head left along the path here, across the reservoir and along the shore back to the car park. There are some carved picnic benches along this shoreline if you want to stop for a rest or a bite to eat, or to just watch the world go by.

Discover Winemaking in Trysull

A splendid escarpment walk taking in a surprisingly successful South Staffordshire vineyard.

46

DISTANCE 5.25 miles (8.4km) **MINIMUM TIME** 1hr 45min

ASCENT/GRADIENT 270ft (82m) ▲▲▲ **LEVEL OF DIFFICULTY** ✦✦✦

PATHS Roads, grass and dirt trails, gravel tracks, 3 stiles

LANDSCAPE Village, farmland and escarpment top

SUGGESTED MAP OS Explorer 219 Wolverhampton & Dudley

START/FINISH Grid reference: SO 852943

DOG FRIENDLINESS Keep on lead near livestock

PARKING Ample street parking in Trysull

PUBLIC TOILETS None en route

The Halfpenny Green Vineyard is situated on the southern-facing slopes of Upper Whittimere, to make the most of the sun throughout the year. The area was first planted in 1983 with the idea of producing wine for personal consumption, but the fine quality of the results led to it becoming a thriving business. Today, an astonishing 50,000 bottles are produced here every year.

It Began With the Romans

The vineyards are one of more than 400 in the UK, most of them in the south of England or South Wales. Winemaking is undoubtedly enjoying something of a revival in this country, thanks largely to improved methods and a rigorous application of science in overcoming the problems of drought, disease and lack of sunshine. Since the Romans cultivated vines here almost 2,000 years ago numerous attempts have been made to make English vineyards a viable alternative to their continental counterparts, but almost without exception these efforts ended in failure.

The British Weather

It wasn't until after World War II that research chemist Ray Barrington Brock set himself the mission of discovering which varieties of grape could cope best with the vagaries of the British weather. His work inspired others to follow suit, and in 1955 the first English wine to be made commercially since World War One went on sale.

Since then, there has been a steady increase in the number of vineyards and labels. In the last decade or so, however, this trend has levelled off, partly because many vineyards were established with little knowledge of the science involved. It was once said that the best way to earn a small fortune was to have a large fortune and buy an English vineyard. Today though, there are numerous thriving vineyards throughout the south, despite the fact that in England only two years in every ten are 'good' years, with four average and four poor, again largely due to problems associated with weather. The most successful vineyards are well-sited with respect to sunlight and soil, grow appropriate varieties for the conditions, and are managed as scientific and commercial enterprises.

Quality Wines

Wines labelled as 'British' are often merely made in the UK from imported wine concentrate and are invariably of poor quality, a fact which goes a little way to explaining the reputation of so-called 'British' wines. To be labelled 'English', wines must be made from grapes grown in England, with the wine itself also made in England. Time was when turning one's nose up at English 'plonk' was justified, but if the wine at Halfpenny Green is anything to go by, domestic wine is now flowing stronger than ever.

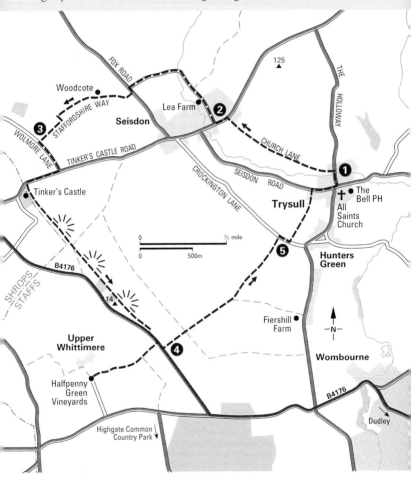

WALK 46 DIRECTIONS

❶ From All Saints Church, head north along The Holloway for 100yds (91m) and, after crossing a small brook, go left along Church Lane as far as Seisdon (this might be muddy after heavy rain). Turn left on to the road (there is no pavement here, so exercise caution), and then take the first turning on the right, called Post Office Road, towards Lea Farm.

2 Follow this road all the way round to a T-junction with Fox Road, heading left then immediately right towards Woodcote. Stay on this track round to the right, following signs for the Staffordshire Way and, at the top of the lane, go through a swing gate to continue along a narrower dirt trail. At the corner of the hedge follow the path left around the edge of the field and then immediately right up to Wolmore Lane.

WHERE TO EAT AND DRINK

The Bell in Trysull is an excellent village pub offering food at lunchtime and in the evening, every day. Bar snacks such as jacket potatoes, pies and baguettes are all served at very reasonable prices, and there's also a full restaurant menu. The interior is friendly and relaxed, while the picnic tables have a fine view of All Saints Church.

3 Head left along this metalled road and then right along Tinker's Castle Road. At the top of the hill, just before Tinker's Castle itself, head left up a path between a wall and a fence. Continue along the edge of the escarpment for 1.25 miles (2km), until it joins the B4176. Just after the junction, head right along a public footpath to visit Halfpenny Green Vineyards (where there's a tea room and restaurant, gift shop and craft centre). To resume the main walk, keep going along the B4176 for 50yds (46m), and turn off left over a stile.

4 Go straight across the middle of the field to a stile and then follow the hedge just to your right in the same direction. At the far right-hand corner of this field keep going straight on, aiming for a tree in the hedge ahead.

WHILE YOU'RE THERE

Highgate Common Country Park, just to the south of Trysull, offers a wide expanse of open heathland and forest, with numerous trails criss-crossing the area and plenty of perfect picnic spots. There are public toilets at the south-west car park.

Go through a wide gap in the hedge and bear slightly left to cross this next field all the way to Crockington Lane. (If this field is impassable because of crops, it may be easier to simply bear right along the hedge to Fiershill Farm, but this means a longer walk along the road into Trysull.)

5 Cross a stile to reach Crockington Lane and then go right for 100yds (91m), before turning left through a kissing gate. Go straight on across this field to the far side and then down a track between houses to Seisdon Road. Turn right here, back to the start.

WHAT TO LOOK OUT FOR

As you walk along Wolmore Lane (see Point **3**), check out the huge holly bushes that have been trimmed and sculpted into the shapes of trees. English holly can grow up to 50ft (15m) or higher, but to ensure berry production, both male and female holly trees need to be planted. This is because the male and female flowers of holly are produced on different plants. In order for bees and other insects to successfully pollinate female flowers, male trees need to be planted within 100ft (30m) or so.

The Wombourne Railway Walk

*A short stroll along a disused railway tracing the
rise and fall of local transport in the area.*

DISTANCE	4.25 miles (6.8km) **MINIMUM TIME** 1hr 30min
ASCENT/GRADIENT	360ft (110m) ▲▲▲ **LEVEL OF DIFFICULTY** +✤✤
PATHS	Roads, gravel and dirt tracks, 4 stiles
LANDSCAPE	Disused railway, meadow and hilltop
SUGGESTED MAP	OS Explorer 219 Wolverhampton & Dudley
START/FINISH	Grid reference: SO 870939
DOG FRIENDLINESS	Must be on lead in fields and on roads
PARKING	Car park off Bratch Lane, Wombourne
PUBLIC TOILETS	None en route

Referred to in the Domesday Book as Womburne, the name Wombourne is thought to mean winding stream (the Anglo-Saxon 'burn' is still used in parts of Scotland and Northumberland to mean a brook). At that time (1086) it was reported as having a population of just 26 people, and by 1641 that number had barely risen above 100. Clearly, this was not a booming town, and despite a number of small industries making their mark on the village in subsequent centuries – agriculture from the 1750s, horticulture around 1800, and sand-mining and nail production from about 1850 onwards – it served as little more than a stop-off on the Staffordshire and Worcestershire Canal throughout this time.

The Canals...
The canal itself was one of the first to be built in Staffordshire, and was designed by engineering genius James Brindley (see Walk 50). Originally it was well-placed for the Potteries, carrying goods to and from Bristol, Gloucester and the West Country via the River Severn. Later, in the 1830s, it faced stiff competition from the Worcestershire and Birmingham Canal and the Birmingham and Liverpool Junction Canal, but despite this setback it continued to make a profit until the 1860s. By then, however, the impact of the railways was beginning to bite, and the canal ceased to be a significant transport route by the turn of the century.

...and the Railways
But, as it turned out, the local railway fared little better, again thanks to competition from bigger, inter-city lines. The South Staffordshire Railway, serving the rural areas to the west of Dudley and Wolverhampton, was owned by Great Western Railways. Building started in 1912, but – due in part to the interruption of World War I – it was not completed until 1925. Right from the start, the line wasn't very successful and passenger services were withdrawn by 1932. During World War II, following the D-Day landings in June of 1944, it was used to transport wounded allied soldiers to hospitals in the area, and after the war it was used for transporting goods.

WOMBOURNE

Following the nationalisation of the railways in 1948, it became a part of the Western Region of what was then British Railways, but the continued decline in traffic during the 1950s and 60s resulted in its inevitable closure. The last train ran in 1965.

The rail company's loss, however, was the public's gain. Today the old line has been converted into a popular walking and cycle path, called the South Staffordshire Railway Walk, through quiet, rolling farmland, the flat, all-weather surface making it ideal for wheelchairs, pushchairs and family cycling. The route along the railway line itself can be extended in either direction by continuing along the Pensnett section in Dudley or the Valley Park section in Wolverhampton.

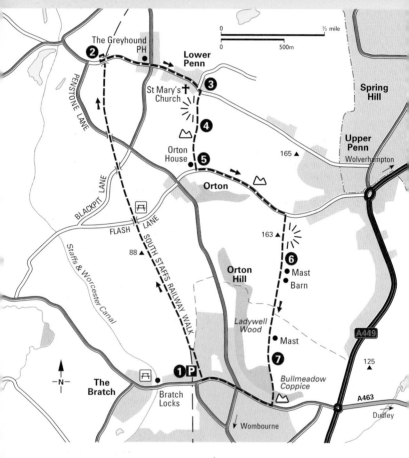

WALK 47 DIRECTIONS

1 From the far end of the car park, walk the few paces onto the disused South Staffordshire Railway line, close to the former station and platform. Head right and continue along a gravel track for 1.5 miles (2.4km), passing over

Flash Lane, Blackpit Lane and Penstone Lane (there are picnic benches either side of Flash Lane if you're in need of rest and refreshment).

2 At the first bridge you go under, turn immediately left up a short track to reach the road, and then head left along the road for 0.5 mile (800m). It's usually quiet along this stretch of road but there are one or two blind corners, so care needs to be taken. Pass The Greyhound pub in Lower Penn on your left, and continue over the crossroads towards Upper Penn.

3 Go past St Mary's Church on your right and, after passing a black-and-white timbered cottage and a barn also on the right, cross right, over a stile following the footpath sign to the kissing gate on the far side of the field. After the gate, follow a grass trail across the next field.

WHILE YOU'RE THERE

Bratch Locks, on the Staffordshire and Worcestershire Canal just west of the start point, are well worth visiting, either for a picnic or just for a quick look around. This three-tiered stair, negotiating a 30ft (9m) rise, is arguably the highlight of Brindley's canal. Two large side ponds were built to accept excess water diverted from the two upper locks.

---

4 At the far side of this field go over a stile and down some steep wooden steps and through a swing gate. Continue along the steep, well-worn trail to reach the bottom of the field (this can get very slippery when wet) before crossing a stile. Stay on the narrow dirt track; it might be thick with greenery in the summer, but there should be an obvious passage through.

5 From Orton House, go left along the narrow, single-track road for 0.5 mile (800m); again, it's very quiet, but take care on blind bends. Follow the road as it steepens up to the top. Just after the brow of the hill, go right along

---

WHERE TO EAT AND DRINK

If the weather's fine then there's no better place to have your lunch than at Bratch Locks picnic site, right by the canal. Failing that, The Round Oak in Wombourne has a beer garden on the canal, not to mention a children's play area, and offers a wide range of hot and cold dishes. It's all standard fare, but the daily specials are excellent value for money.

---

a wide track (a public bridleway) past several houses. This hedge-lined route offers great views of the rolling green hills of the Black Country to the east.

6 Follow the track to the right of the communications mast and a large concrete and steel barn, and continue down a wide track to the right. When the track goes hard left, cross over a stile ahead and continue in the same direction across the middle of the field to the corner of Bullmeadow Coppice, veering left at the end.

7 Follow the path to an open meadow, then go straight on along the edge of the wood to the corner. Here go right for a narrow path down the steep and sometimes slippery hillside. Turn right, when you reach the road, and go straight over at a crossroads to return to the car park at the start.

WHAT TO LOOK OUT FOR

Towards the end of the walk, see if you can spot the tower of Wombourne village church. Although the 14th-century building is of little interest architecturally, it's thought to be unique in its dedication to Saint Biscop, a Benedictine monk born in AD 628 and famed for his travels and the pictures and manuscripts he collected en route.

Kinver's Impressive Rock Houses

*A short walk combining curious cave dwellings
with some of the best views in Staffordshire.*

DISTANCE 2.75 miles (4.4km)   **MINIMUM TIME** 1hr

ASCENT/GRADIENT 374ft (114m) ▲▲▲   **LEVEL OF DIFFICULTY** ◆◆◆

PATHS Wide gravel tracks and dirt paths

LANDSCAPE Woodland and escarpment top

SUGGESTED MAP OS Explorer 219 Wolverhampton & Dudley

START/FINISH Grid reference: SO 835836

DOG FRIENDLINESS Can be taken off lead

PARKING Verge-side parking on Compton Road, Kinver

PUBLIC TOILETS None en route

The impressive sandstone ridge to the south-west of Kinver has been occupied in one way or another since 2500 BC, and impressive earthworks, believed to have been built at around this time, still exist near the summit.

Kinver Edge

The views from the summit, and in fact along the length of Kinver Edge, are indeed tremendous, and it must have seemed an impressive vantage point on which to build defences. Today, a brass relief map at the north end (Point ❷), presented by the local Rotary Club in 1990, points to a selection of the world's major capitals, in addition to less distant landmarks. Both the Malvern Hills, 30 miles (48km) to the south, and Long Mynd, the same distance to the west, are visible on a clear day and, at times, it may be possible to see the Black Mountains, over 45 miles (72km) away. But for all its breathtaking views, the real interest on Kinver Edge lies below the summit, in small houses carved into the rock.

Holy Austin Rock

Of these, by far the most impressive are the dwellings at Holy Austin Rock, a short walk to the east of the car park. Legend has it that it was named after a hermit who lived near the site. The first written reference to people actually living in houses cut out of the rock face is believed to be in a book about a walk in the area, written in 1777. The author, seeking shelter from a storm, encounters 'this exceedingly curious rock inhabited by a clean and decent family', before going on to describe the rooms as 'really curious, warm and commodious'.

Family Homes

By the beginning of the 19th century there were several rock houses, and for the next 100 years or so they were permanently occupied. By 1861 there were 11 families in residence, the increase almost certainly due to the demand created by the local iron works. When these went into decline at the end of the 19th century, the houses were gradually abandoned, although two families continued to live there until the end of World War II, and the last occupants didn't move out until 1963. A tourist café also lasted until 1967, after which the houses fell into decline and neglect: vandalism led to collapses and, sadly, one area had to be destroyed for safety reasons.

Postcard Plans

It wasn't until the 1980s that plans were finally drawn up to renovate the houses to their original state, a task which was achieved with the help of postcards popular 100 years earlier. The rebuilding was completed in 1993 and the site was again occupied, this time by a National Trust custodian. While this house is private, the rest of the site is open to the public all year-round. The lower rock houses are only open on weekend afternoons

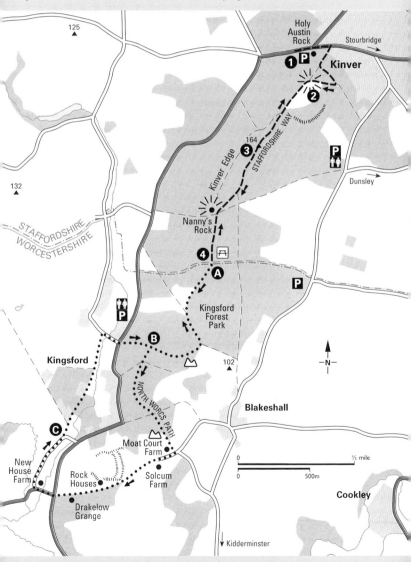

between March and the end of November (2–4pm). Visitors can see how occupants would have lived 100 or so years ago, and may be surprised at just how cosy the houses feel. The combination of thick sandstone and fireplaces would have kept them warm in winter and cool in summer, whilst in many places interior walls were plastered and whitewashed. Today, Holy Austin Rock has also been designated as a Site of Special Scientific Interest (SSSI) for its sandstone, which was formed from solidified sand dunes in the Permian era, 250 million years ago.

WALK 48 DIRECTIONS

1 From the wide roadside car parking, head back along the road towards Kinver village. Within 100yds (91m), after going right at a fork in the road, follow public footpath signs to the right, up into the woods. Once you're in the woods proper, take the obvious path left to the small clearing and then turn 90 degrees to the right to follow the short, steep path to the viewpoint.

2 From the viewpoint, continue along the top of the escarpment, following a wide, gravel track running more or less alongside the western edge of the ancient rectangular earthworks to the left, with glimpsed views across the Severn Valley through trees to the right. When the clearing ends, continue on the wide and well-walked track through intermittent woodland, with new and distant views opening up on either side. Carry on along the escarpment top, past the trig point.

3 Staying on the highest path, continue as far as the National Trust boundary gate and continue straight along the main track avoiding smaller trails off to the left and right. The path descends gradually to a small clearing at the entrance to the Forest Park, with signs for the Staffordshire Way and the North Worcestershire Path. A narrow track to the right leads back down to the road and a public toilet if required, although it criss-crosses other paths and it's very easy to lose your bearings!

WHERE TO EAT AND DRINK

The Vine has a beer garden right on the canal at Dunsley and is ideal for children and families in the summer, when you can eat outside. The menu includes chargrill specials, a changing à la carte choice and a Sunday roast.

4 For this reason, it's easiest to return the way you came. From the path junction, head back along the escarpment to the viewpoint. At the end, head right and then left, back down to the clearing, and then left again down the wooden steps, through the trees to the road. Follow the road left as far as the car park. For those armed with the relevant OS map, there is a suitable alternative which returns via the forested slopes to the west of the ridge top, but because of the number of little tracks that cross back and forth, it's difficult to give adequate directions here.

WHAT TO LOOK OUT FOR

Nanny's Rock, just inside the National Trust boundary, and just off the path, provides a breathtaking viewpoint and a great place for a picnic – it, too, has a collection of simple cave or rock dwellings carved out beneath, although considerable care should be taken to reach them as the ground is a bit steep and rocky.

KINVER

Worcestershire Loop

*Extend the walk to take in an ancient fort
and some additional rock houses.*
See map and information panel for Walk 48

DISTANCE 6 miles (9.7km) **MINIMUM TIME** 2hrs 15min
ASCENT/GRADIENT 750ft (229m) ▲▲▲ **LEVEL OF DIFFICULTY** ✦✦✧

WALK 49 DIRECTIONS
(Walk 48 option)

From Point **Ⓐ**, continue along the escarpment, keeping to the main (higher) track and following waymarkers for the North Worcestershire Path. Just past a small, fenced-off water treatment area, turn right, then left, and follow the waymarked path to a junction on the edge of the wood. Go right, down a fairly steep path.

Where this path meets a wooden barrier and a more obvious sand track at right angles, Point **Ⓑ**, head left. After 300yds (274m) you come to another path junction. Take the smallest, central path, following the yellow arrow. On reaching a sandy track go straight over, coming shortly to a steep hill. When you get to the clearing at the top, cross the stile and continue in the same direction, with a fence to your left. In the far left corner of the field, go through a gate on to the road.

Head right towards Solcum Farm, passing Moat Court Farm on the right and, shortly after, Solcum Farm on the left. Head to the right of Solcum Farm following a succession of yellow arrows down a dark and heavily wooded track past Drakelow Grange. At the crossroads continue straight on and take the first right at New House Farm. Carry on to where the surfaced road turns to the right and follow the track off left, Point **Ⓒ**.

WHAT TO LOOK OUT FOR

As you descend into the dark woods beyond Solcum Farm, the steep bank to the right forms the remains of some Iron Age earthworks not unlike the one at the start of the walk. Just before you get to the recently built Drakelow Grange, turn right off the main path up a dirt track to reach another group of rock houses. These are far less developed than those at Kinver, which makes them all the more appealing, as it's possible to wander into different rooms.

Immediately after Point **Ⓒ**, take the right fork and, when the track turns left, continue straight on to the right of the fence, following the yellow arrows. Just after crossing a stile, turn right along the metalled road until it meets a bigger road. Go straight across and up a footpath just to the left, by a Forest Park sign. When this path meets a wide sand bridleway (Point **Ⓑ** again), continue across and back up the way you came, retracing your steps back to the start.

Kinver's Rise and Fall

50

*Celebrating a success story and remembering
a tragedy on this final walk.*

DISTANCE 3.25 miles (5.3km)	**MINIMUM TIME** 1hr 15min
ASCENT/GRADIENT 360ft (110m) ▲▲	**LEVEL OF DIFFICULTY** +++
PATHS Grass tracks, field paths, roads and dirt trails, 20 stiles	
LANDSCAPE Field, meadow, woodland and canalside	
SUGGESTED MAP OS Explorer 219 Wolverhampton & Dudley	
START/FINISH Grid reference: SO 848835	
DOG FRIENDLINESS Keep on lead in all fields	
PARKING Roadside in Kinver village	
PUBLIC TOILETS None en route	

WALK 50 DIRECTIONS

Given the part canals have played in the Staffordshire landscape over the past 250 years, it seems appropriate that the final walk in the book should include at least a short section of artificial waterway, even if it isn't the walk's highlight.

It seems fitting too, that the Staffordshire and Worcestershire Canal was designed and built under the apparently omnipotent eye of James Brindley, whose name is associated with so many of the walks in this volume, and who perhaps did more than any other single person to shape the landscape and fortune of the county.

The Staffordshire and Worcester Canal was one of Brindley's earliest projects; it was officially opened in 1772. Essentially, it was part of his so-called 'Grand Cross', a visionary scheme to connect all of the major ports (Bristol, Hull and Liverpool) by linking the Severn, the Trent and the Mersey. The canal begins at the River Severn before rising slowly to Aldersley Junction,

near Wolverhampton, where it connects with the Shropshire Union Canal (see Walk 35). It then continues as far as the Trent and Mersey Canal at Great Haywood near Shugborough (see Walk 33); its highlight has to be the three-tier lock at The Bratch, near Wombourne (see Walk 47).

However, despite James Brindley's best efforts, the highlight of this walk has to be The Whittington Inn, a timber-beamed manor house built in 1310 that now serves a very reasonable pint. Originally owned by Sir William de Whittington, then owner and lord of all Kinver, it was later inherited by ancestors of Lady Jane Grey, who's reported to have spent some of her childhood here, before her life was plunged into turmoil. She

WHERE TO EAT AND DRINK

The Whittington Inn is the obvious place to feast and imbibe, either during the walk or afterwards. An extensive menu is served in cosy, immaculate surroundings, all day.

was fourth in line to the throne in Henry VIII's will, but thanks to the scheming by her Protestant father-in-law, a royal advisor, she was crowned Queen ahead of Mary, who was Catholic. She ruled for just nine days, before Mary, with strong popular support, seized the throne and had her imprisoned in the Tower of London. Less than a year later, aged just 16, she was beheaded. Later, during the reign of Mary's successor, Queen Elizabeth I, Jane was celebrated as a Protestant martyr. Today, her ghost is said to still haunt the inn.

WHAT TO LOOK OUT FOR

50

The 14th-century front door of the Whittington bears Queen Anne's seal, with the inscription Anne R. 1711, indicating that she stayed here on one of her royal trips. It's thought that this is one of only two of her seals in existence.

From the Vine pub, go left uphill for 100yds (91m) and then right along a gravel track ('Gibraltar') between houses. Just after some cottages on your left, go left at a fork, up the steep hill to the corner of a driveway (you'll return here later). Go left and then immediately right here, just after Dunsley House, along a wide dirt and grass track.

Cross a stile and continue along the well-trodden grass trail, following the fence just to your right. At the brow of the hill cross over a stile with an ingenious 'paddle' gate for dogs. Cross the middle of a grass meadow to a high stile on the far side. Continue straight across the middle of a series of fields, crossing stiles into each to reach the A449.

Take great care crossing this busy road, and then head left for 100yds (91m), then right, over a stile. Follow the fence-side path next to a newly planted area of trees up to the corner of Gibbet Wood on the hilltop. Cross the stile and go right, along the edge of the wood to another stile and then veer left to reach Gibbet Lane. Head right here for 350yds (320m) and right again over a stile in the high, barbed-wire topped metal fence. Cross the

private access road, another stile, and continue into the next field.

At the bottom of the field go right along a tree-lined track. At the end of these trees, cross a stile and continue along a fence to your right for 100yds (91m). As the fence bears round to the right, keep going straight to the stile in the fence ahead. Cross this stile and head straight across the middle of the next grass field, contouring around until you reach a stile in the middle of the fence on the far side. Bear slightly left across another field to a gate, and then cut off the corner of the next field to another gate. After this gate you shortly come to another stile and gate. Cross this stile and follow the left-hand edge of the field all the way to a stile on to the A449 at The Whittington Inn.

Go straight over the busy road here (taking great care) and follow the footpath sign to Lower Whittington. Take the trail down the back of some houses and, at the road, go right, following the footpath sign to a swing gate and the canal.

Follow the canal to the kissing gate into woods and continue through the woods and past some impressive canal-front homes. At a fork just after these houses go right up a hill to return to the driveway passed earlier. From here, retrace your steps back to the start.

Walking in Safety

All these walks are suitable for any reasonably fit person, but less experienced walkers should try the easier walks first. Route finding is usually straightforward, but you will find that an Ordnance Survey map is a useful addition to the route maps and descriptions.

RISKS

Although each walk here has been researched with a view to minimising the risks to the walkers who follow its route, no walk in the countryside can be considered to be completely free from risk. Walking in the outdoors will always require a degree of common sense and judgement to ensure that it is as safe as possible.

● Be particularly careful on cliff paths and in upland terrain, where the consequences of a slip can be very serious.

● Remember to check tidal conditions before walking on the seashore.

● Some sections of route are by, or cross, busy roads. Take care and remember traffic is a danger even on minor country lanes.

● Be careful around farmyard machinery and livestock, especially if you have children with you.

● Be aware of the consequences of changes in the weather and check the forecast before you set out. Carry spare clothing and a torch if you are walking in the winter months. Remember the weather can change very quickly at any time of the year, and in moorland and heathland areas, mist and fog can make route finding much harder. Don't set out in these conditions unless you are confident of your navigation skills in poor visibility. In summer remember to take account of the heat and sun; wear a hat and carry spare water.

● On walks away from centres of population you should carry a whistle and survival bag. If you do have an accident requiring the emergency services, make a note of your position as accurately as possible and dial 999.

COUNTRYSIDE CODE

● Be safe, plan ahead and follow any signs.
● Leave gates and property as you find them.
● Protect plants and animals and take your litter home.
● Keep dogs under close control.
● Consider other people.

For more information visit www.countrysideaccess.gov.uk/things_to_know/countryside_code